DOMESTIC VIOLENCE
STOPS WITH YOU

AVAILABLE CIVIL REMEDIES
IN ILLINOIS

@ Sterk Family Law Group

Empower Yourself With Options

Domestic Violence Stops With You
Available Civil Remedies in Illinois

Written By
Sterk Family Law Group, P.C.

Contributing Authors
Alyssa A. Blando

Amy M. Bravo

Amanda N. Engelman

Arianna A. Fleckenstein

Terrence M. Fogarty

Kelly L. Garver

Jennifer J. Hanik

Laura A. Kennard

Kelli M. Lardi

Nicole L. Morales

Jennifer S. Nolen

Ragan Pattison

Crystal S. Pavloski

Amy A. Schellekens

Frederick M. Smithhart

Gwendolyn J. Sterk

Jackie L. Sulich

Joan van Oss

Monika L. Wolniak

Book Layout & Design
K.P. Lynne

ISBN: 978-1-7357148-4-4

Koru
Legal Publishing, LLC

Gwendolyn J. Sterk and the Family Law Group

Gwendolyn J. Sterk has been practicing family law since 1989 and founded Sterk Family Law Group, P.C. in 2015 in Orland Park, Illinois. Built on a mission to educate, empower, and equip, the firm takes a holistic approach to the practice of family law and estate planning. The Sterk Family Law team believes legal support should go hand in hand with emotional and personal guidance, working to meet clients where they are and support their growth through life's most challenging transitions.

More than just legal professionals, the team has built a network of counselors, support groups, and non-traditional service providers to offer clients access to tools that help them prepare for their next steps. This approach is reflected in the firm's unique Resource Center, which serves as a bridge between legal services and real-life needs.

In their continued commitment to community education, the firm actively shares knowledge through speaking engagements with local chambers, mental health organizations, and schools. Sterk Family Law Group also offers free educational content through their Resource Sessions podcast and YouTube channel, where Gwendolyn J. Sterk and guest professionals explore topics ranging from legal updates to mental health, finances, and family dynamics.

This book is another resource designed to help you feel informed, supported, and confident. Whether you are navigating divorce, allocating parental responsibilities, or preparing an estate plan, we hope this information helps guide you forward with integrity and dignity.

- The Sterk Family Law Group Team

Helpful Resources

Call 911 if You Are in Immediate Danger

Sterk Family Law Group, P.C.
www.sterkfamilylaw.com
info@sterkfamilylaw.com
1-815-600-8950
Connect on Facebook, YouTube, LinkedIn, Spotify, Instagram: Sterk Family Law Group
Serving Illinois Clients in Cook, Will, DuPage and Kane County

National Domestic Violence Hotline

800.799.SAFE (7233)
https://www.thehotline.org/

Illinois Department of Human Services Domestic Violence Helpline

1-877-TO END DV or 1-877-863-6338 (Voice)
1-877-863-6339 (TTY)
The hotline is toll free, confidential, multilingual, and open 24-hours.

Crisis Center for South Suburbia 24 Hour Hotline

708-429-7233
https://crisisctr.org/contact/

Table of Contents

DOMESTIC VIOLENCE IS SERIOUS

There is no particular social class, economic class, gender, race, or ethnicity who is exempt from domestic violence. Domestic violence is not limited to one certain class of individuals who are more prone to violence and there is no particular stereotype. It occurs in affluent families as well as families below the poverty line. Regardless of your background, the law affords the same opportunities for protection to all victims of domestic violence.

Domestic Violence is an epidemic that affects an unknown number of people due to the underreported nature of the issue. This abuse comes in many forms: physical abuse, mental abuse, verbal abuse, spiritual abuse, sexual abuse, and financial abuse. It is estimated that 1.3 million women and 835,000 men are victims of physical violence by an intimate partner each year. *Intimate Partner Violence - Statistics*, EXHALE TO INHALE, https://www.exhaletoinhale.org/dv-statistics (last visited June 23, 2020).

The National Coalition Against Domestic Violence reports that 85% of victims are women and it is believed that one in every four American women will experience or has experienced Domestic Violence in their lifetime. *Id.* For many, their home is a place of warmth, comfort and stability. It is also the place they feel safe. Most people enjoy time with their families inside their home and have a place to decompress from the hustle of life. For Domestic Violence victims, a home is the opposite of that; it is more like a prison. Because Domestic Violence is a taboo social topic, many people go to great lengths to hide what is happening inside their residence. Instead of disclosing the abuse to family and loved ones, victims become isolated from the people that were close to them in the past.

Domestic Violence has many ripple effects on a victim's life. These effects can be emotional and psychological and can continue long after the abuse has ended. Victims experience fear for their safety, fear for the safety of others, and suffer emotional distress. Many victims alter their daily routines to avoid the persons who are abusing them. Some victims are in such fear that they relocate to another city, town or state. Depending on the connections between the victim and their abuser, the lingering effects of the abuse can evoke many troublesome feelings for the victim.

Due to the commonly reported feelings of shame and guilt, a victim may continue to isolate themselves from loved ones and have issues with poverty and homelessness due to past abusive acts. The connections they may have had in the past may have been eroded or the abuse victim believes the relationships are eroded and they have no one to turn to for help or support. Additionally, survivors of domestic violence have the scars of past abuse significantly influencing their potential for future romantic relationships. Some survivors, looking for a loving relationship, enter into new relationships which duplicate the same patterns of abuse.

Domestic violence is not a subject to be taken lightly. Domestic violence is a crime. In fact, Section 102 of the Illinois Domestic Violence Act of 1986 (herein IDVA), specifically identifies domestic violence as a serious crime against both the individual as well as society. 750 Ill. Comp. Stat. Ann. 60/102(1) (LexisNexis through P.A. 101-631). The IDVA was enacted to promote the underlying purpose of recognizing domestic violence as a serious crime against the individual and society which produces family disharmony in thousands of Illinois families, promotes a pattern of escalating violence which frequently culminates in intra-family homicide, and creates an emotional atmosphere that is not conducive to healthy childhood development.

It also recognizes domestic violence against high-risk adults with disabilities, who are particularly vulnerable due to impairments in ability to seek or obtain protection, as a serious problem which takes on many forms, including physical abuse, sexual abuse, neglect, and exploitation. Finally, the IDVA facilitates accessibility of remedies under the Act in order to provide immediate and effective assistance and protection. 750 Ill. Comp. Stat. Ann. 60/102(1)-(2) (LexisNexis through P.A. 101-631).

The IDVA also seeks to support the efforts of victims of domestic violence to avoid further abuse by promptly entering and diligently enforcing court orders which prohibit abuse and, when necessary, reduce the abuser's access to the victim and address any related issues of child custody and economic support, so that victims are not trapped in abusive situations by fear of retaliation, loss of a child, financial dependence, or loss of accessible housing or services. 750 Ill. Comp. Stat. Ann. 60/102(4) (LexisNexis through P.A. 101-631).

The Illinois Domestic Violence Act of 1986 also defines the terms of domestic violence and abuse. Domestic violence is defined as the abuse by a family or household member. The term abuse has been defined as physical abuse, harassment, intimidation of a dependent, interference with the personal liberty, neglect, or willful deprivation. 750 Ill. Comp. Stat. Ann. 60/103(1) (LexisNexis through P.A. 101-631). In recognizing that the legal system was once ineffective when dealing with family violence, the legislators enacted the Illinois Domestic Violence Act of 1986 to avoid the widespread failure to appropriately protect and assist victims of domestic violence.

A recent addition to the Illinois Domestic Violence Act of 1986 is the Victims' Economic Security & Safety Act (VESSA). In previous years, victims of domestic violence found it difficult to seek necessary services for fear of taking too much time off work in order to pursue remedies for domestic violence. As a result of the fear of missing work or losing a job, as of January 1, 2017, employers must allow time off from work for victims of domestic violence in order for the victims to seek medical attention, obtain victim services and/or counseling, seek legal assistance to ensure safety, and to participate in court proceedings related to the violence alleged. 820 Ill. Comp. Stat. Ann. 180/20(a)(1)(A)-(E) (LexisNexis through P.A. 101-631).

VESSA provides for penalties for an employer's failure to implement and follow the procedures as enumerated in VESSA. The Department of Labor is the regulatory agency who will conduct any investigations as to any reported violations of VESSA. 820 Ill. Comp. Stat. Ann. 180/35(a)(1) (LexisNexis through P.A. 101-631). Such penalties include, but are not limited to, paying reasonable attorneys' fees and compensation for lost wages. 820 Ill. Comp. Stat. Ann. 180/35(a)(1)(A)-(C) (LexisNexis through P.A. 101-631).

Illinois has taken measures to include salon professionals in the fight against domestic violence. As of January 1, 2017. Illinois became the first state in the nation to require that hair stylists attend domestic violence training. 225 Ill. Comp. Stat. Ann. 410/3-7 (LexisNexis through P.A. 101-631). This training is to help salon professionals recognize the potential victims of domestic violence and sexual assault. The law does not require salon professionals to become mandatory reporters, but the law urges the professionals to assist and direct their clients to domestic violence resources.

The Illinois Domestic Violence Act ("IDVA") is a law that relates specifically to family and household members. Under the IDVA, a Circuit Court Judge can order and forbid a family or household member from continuous abusive behavior by granting an Order of Protection. Whether you are the person seeking an Order of Protection or the individual who is ordered to comply, it is extremely important to understand the severity and obligations of such an Order.

An Order of Protection is a written Court Order which prohibits abusive behavior by law. The Order is protective by nature and usually requires that the alleged abuser stay away from the victim and cease all contact with him or her. The IDVA considers various behaviors as abusive including physical abuse, harassment, intimidation of a dependent, interference with personal liberty, willful deprivation, exploitation, and stalking. 750 Ill. Comp. Stat. Ann. 60/103(a) (LexisNexis through P.A. 101-631). These types of restraining Orders are only put in place after a Judge deems it necessary. It is imperative to understand the Order and to comply with the restrictions outlined therein. Anyone found to be in violation of an Order of Protection will find themselves in a legal position much worse than that which required the Order in the first place.

Orders of Protection can be entered to protect a spouse, an ex-spouse, a girlfriend/boyfriend who have or have had a dating or engagement relationship, parents, children, stepchildren, significant other/partner, persons who share or allege a blood relationship through a child, persons who live together or formerly lived together and persons with disabilities and their personal assistants.

Illinois Domestic Violence Act, Section 201(a) specifies who is eligible for an Order of Protection. 750 Ill. Comp. Stat. Ann. 60/201(a) (LexisNexis through P.A. 101-631). What you should remember is that eligibility does not mean that you will automatically be granted an Order of Protection by an Illinois court.

The provisions of the Act provide that the following persons are eligible for protection by the Act:

1. *Any person abused by a family or household member;*
2. *Any high-risk adult with disabilities who is abused, neglected, or exploited by a family or household member;*
3. *Any minor child or dependent adult in the care of such person; and*
4. *Any person residing or employed at a private home or public shelter which is housing an abused family or household member.*

750 Ill. Comp. Stat. Ann. 60/201(a)(i)-(iv) (LexisNexis through P.A. 101-631).

An Order of Protection can protect victims of abuse, minors, or dependent adults in their care, and anyone who lives at or is employed at their place of residence. *Id.* In order to obtain an Order of Protection, allegations of some form of abuse need to be made by the party seeking the Emergency Order of Protection (or the Petitioner). 750 Ill. Comp. Stat. Ann. 60/203(a) (LexisNexis through P.A. 101-631). The allegations can include descriptions of physical abuse, harassment, intimidation of a dependent, interference with personal liberty, or willful deprivation. If someone does not meet the criteria for an Order of Protection, a Stalking No Contact Order is another option for relief. 740 Ill. Comp. Stat. Ann. 21/15 (LexisNexis through P.A. 101-650). The statute provides that the following persons are eligible for a Stalking No Contact Order:

1. *Any person who is a victim of stalking;*
2. *A person on behalf of a minor child or an adult who is a victim of stalking, but because of age, disability, health, or inaccessibility, cannot file the petition;*
3. *An authorized agent of a workplace;*
4. *An authorized agent of a place or worship; or*
5. *An authorized agent of a school.*

740 Ill. Comp. Stat. Ann. 21/15(1)-(5) (LexisNexis through P.A. 101-650).

Under the Illinois Stalking No Contact Order Act, stalking is defined as engaging in a court of conduct directed at a specific person, and he or she knows or should know that this course of conduct would cause a reasonable person to fear for his or her safety, the safety of a workplace, school, or place of worship, or the safety of a third person or suffer emotional distress. 740 Ill. Comp. Stat. Ann. 21/10 (LexisNexis through P.A. 101-650). "Course of conduct" means two or more acts, including but not limited to acts in which a respondent directly, indirectly, or through third parties, by any action, method, or means follows, monitors, observes, surveils, or threatens a person, workplace, school, or place of worship, engages in other contact, or interferes with or damages a person's property or pet. *Id.* It also includes contact via electronic means. *Id.* But, stalking does not include an exercise of the right to free speech or assembly that is otherwise lawful or picketing occurring at a workplace that is otherwise lawful and arises out of a bona fide labor dispute. *Id.*

4

Forms of Abuse

Physical abuse can be defined as any act using physical force, confinement, or restraint against another person. 750 Ill. Comp. Stat. Ann. 60/103(14)(i) (LexisNexis through P.A. 101-631). Physical abuse also includes sexual abuse, sleep deprivation, and creating an immediate risk of physical harm. 750 Ill. Comp. Stat. Ann. 60/103(14)(ii)-(iii) (LexisNexis through P.A. 101-631). The evidence of physical abuse shows up in bruises, broken bones, cuts, scars, blackened eyes, and open wounds. The court can visibly see some signs of physical abuse. Be sure to document the evidence of physical abuse. Take pictures and video upon the first appearance of any signs of physical abuse. Document the attack and the areas attacked with a physician.

Harassment means knowing, unnecessary, and unreasonable conduct that is causing emotional distress. 750 Ill. Comp. Stat. Ann. 60/103(7) (LexisNexis through P.A. 101-631). Some examples of harassing behavior include but are not limited to making a disturbance at work or school, repeated calls or texts, threatening suicide, or threatening physical violence, confinement, or restraint. 750 Ill. Comp. Stat. Ann. 60/103(7)(i), (ii), and (vi) (LexisNexis through P.A. 101-631).

Also, snatching a child or repeatedly threatening to do so is a harassing behavior. 750 Ill. Comp. Stat. Ann. 60/103(7)(v) (LexisNexis through P.A. 101-631). The key to understanding harassment is to evaluate whether the conduct is unreasonable and whether the conduct causes emotional distress.

There have been cases where an abuser calls a victim more than 100 times every day just to get the victim to "talk" to them and work things out. Granted, the reason for the call may have seemed innocent enough to the abuser, but the excessive calling is unreasonable conduct. Repeated and excessive calls can lead to emotional distress and the feeling that the calls will never end unless you do something about it.

Stalking occurs when a person knowingly engages in two or more acts of surveillance and monitoring of a specific person, and he or she knows or should know that this course of conduct would cause a reasonable person to fear for his or her safety or the safety of a third person; or suffer other emotional distress. 720 Ill. Comp. Stat. Ann. 5/12-7.3(a-3)(1)-(2) (LexisNexis through P.A. 101-631).

Stalking generally refers to a course of conduct, not a single act. 720 Ill. Comp. Stat. Ann. 6/12-7.3(c)(1) (LexisNexis through P.A. 101-631). The course of action could be direct, indirect, or through third parties. *Id.* Stalking actions may include a method, device, or other means in order to follow, monitor, observe, surveil, threaten, or communicate to or about who the abuser is stalking. *Id.* If a person engages in other non-consensual contact or interferes with or damages a person's property or pet, the action could be stalking if the same is under surveillance. *Id.*

Stalking behavior includes following a person, conducting surveillance of the person, appearing at the person's home, work or school, making unwanted phone calls, sending unwanted emails, unwanted messages via social media, or text messages, leaving objects for the person, vandalizing the person's property, or injuring a pet. 740 ILCS 21/5 (LexisNexis through P.A. 101-631).

While estimates suggest that 70% of victims know the individuals stalking them, only 30% of victims have dated or been in intimate relationships with their stalkers. *Id.* All stalking victims should be able to seek a civil remedy requiring the offenders stay away from the victims and third parties. Illinois statute has expanded protections to include Cyberstalking as a form of abuse, and the use of electronic communication as a way to follow and surveil a victim. *Id.*

Be careful before you go out and hire that private investigator to surveille your significant other or household member. You may believe that you are gathering information in order to get back at your cheating spouse. But, by the above definition, you could be stalking.

Interference with personal liberty includes forcing someone to do things that they would not normally do through actual (or the threat of) physical force, abuse, harassment, intimidation or willful deprivation. 750 Ill. Comp. Stat. Ann. 60/103(9) (LexisNexis through P.A. 101-631).

Intimidation of a dependent means involving or engaging in physical abuse of another in front of a dependent. 750 Ill. Comp. Stat. Ann. 60/103(10) (LexisNexis through P.A. 101-631). Willful deprivation is defined as willfully denying someone the care they need due to their disability, age, or health. 750 Ill. Comp. Stat. Ann. 60/103(15) (LexisNexis through P.A. 101-631). Examples of such deprivation include depriving the abused of food, shelter, medical care, and physical help. *Id.*

Neglect is defined as the failure to exercise a reasonable person's degree of care towards a high-risk adult with disabilities and includes: failure to take appropriate measures to protect against abuse; failure to provide food, shelter, clothing, and personal hygiene; failure to provide appropriate medical intervention; and failure to protect for health and safety hazards. 750 Ill. Comp. Stat. Ann. 60/103(11)(A)(i), (iii), (iv), and (v) (LexisNexis through P.A. 101-631). Neglect can also include repeated careless imposition of unreasonable confinement. 750 Ill. Comp. Stat. Ann. 60/103(11)(A)(ii) (LexisNexis through P.A. 101-631).

Exploitation includes but is not limited to, the misappropriation of assets or resources of a high-risk adult with disabilities by undue influence, by breach of a fiduciary relationship, by fraud, deception, or extortion, or the use of such assets or resources in a manner contrary to law. 750 Ill. Comp. Stat. Ann. 60/103(5) (LexisNexis through P.A. 101-631).

The Process

Under the Illinois Domestic Violence Act, there are three types of Orders of Protection. The Orders of Protection include Emergency Order of Protection, Interim Order of Protection, and Plenary Order of Protection. Each of the aforementioned Orders of Protection have special conditions and vary as to the length of time the order of protection is in place after entry.

An Emergency Order of Protection (EOP) is an ex-parte order that can be granted for a period of 14 to 21 days without notice to the abuser (Respondent). 750 Ill. Comp. Stat. Ann. 60/220(a)(1) (LexisNexis through P.A. 101-631). This order may include a provision requiring the Respondent to stay away and have no contact with the Petitioner (the abused party). 750 Ill. Comp. Stat. Ann. 60/217(a)(3)(i) (LexisNexis through P.A. 101-631).

Other provisions may also be included at the discretion of the Judge. In order to obtain an EOP, a Petitioner must be able to demonstrate specific abusive conduct by a Respondent. 750 Ill. Comp. Stat. Ann. 60/217(a)(2) (LexisNexis through P.A. 101-631). The EOP will likely list specific allegations of abusive conduct. These allegations will be the "facts" which will be presented at the hearing for an EOP.

An Interim Order of Protection is an order that can be granted and remain in place for a period of up to 30 days. 750 Ill. Comp. Stat. Ann. 60/220(a)(2) (LexisNexis through P.A. 101-631). Typically, this is used to extend the EOP to give parties time to get ready for a full hearing to determine the need for a Plenary Order of Protection. A Plenary Order of Protection can be granted for up to a two-year period only after a hearing or agreement of the parties. 750 Ill. Comp. Stat. Ann. 60/220(b)(0.05) (LexisNexis through P.A. 101-631). A hearing must be held with both parties having been afforded the opportunity to either obtain legal counsel and/or present evidence and witnesses in court. 750 Ill. Comp. Stat. Ann. 60/219 (LexisNexis through P.A. 101-631).

The process for obtaining an Order of Protection begins with the filing of a Petition for Order of Protection. 750 Ill. Comp. Stat. Ann. 60/202(a)(1) (LexisNexis through P.A. 101-631). The process can be initiated online in Will and DuPage County but must be verified and signed prior to appearing before a Judge. In other counties in Illinois, you will need to appear in person or research local rules for filing.

The Petition must include past and current proceedings between the parties as well as a detailed timeline of abuse that occurred by the abuser. 750 Ill. Comp. Stat. Ann. 60/203(a) (LexisNexis through P.A. 101-631). It is important to remember when preparing the Petition, the victim will be expected to testify about the allegations plead in their Petition for Order of Protection; and therefore, the allegations must be true, accurate and complete, otherwise issues may arise at the hearing.

Untrue statements, allegations and denials, made without reasonable cause and found to be untrue, shall subject the party pleading them to the payment of reasonable expenses actually incurred by the other party by reason of the untrue pleading, together with reasonable attorney's fees to be summarily taxed by the court upon motion made within 30 days of the judgment or dismissal, as provided in Supreme Court Rule 137. 750 Ill. Comp. Stat. Ann. 60/226 (LexisNexis through P.A. 101-631). The court may direct that a copy of an order entered under this Section be provided to the State's Attorney so that he or she may determine whether to prosecute for perjury. *Id.* This Section shall not apply to proceedings heard in Criminal Court or to criminal contempt of court proceedings, whether heard in Civil or Criminal Court. *Id*

Filing for an Order of Protection (OP) is typically a very stressful process. Someone in a position to file for an OP should consider a variety of things based on their specific situation and the domestic abuse that occurred.

First, it is important to realize that the period immediately following the filing of an OP is the most dangerous because it signifies to an abuser that the victim is taking steps to leave the relationship. Therefore, remembering that filing (and obtaining) an OP is the first important step in the process of getting away from an abuser, but preparing for what comes next is just as important.

When filing an OP, it is important to remember each county is different. The county where you choose to file the OP must meet one of four criteria; (1) the victim lives in that county, (2) the abuser lives in that county, (3) the abuse took place in the county, or (4) the OP is filed in the county the victim fled to for their protection. 750 Ill. Comp. Stat. Ann. 60/209(a) (LexisNexis through P.A. 101-631). One option to start the process of obtaining an OP is to complete certain forms online (such as the "Petition for Order of Protection"); i.e. the document wherein the specifics of the alleged abuse are outlined.

The Petition may exclude the petitioner's address if there is fear that the disclosure may further risk the safety of the petitioner or any family member. 750 Ill. Comp. Stat. Ann. 60/203(b) (LexisNexis through P.A. 101-631). However, an alternate address must be provided. *Id.* An address for the Respondent (abuser) is vital to the process. The county sheriff department is responsible for serving the Respondent with a summons and without a viable address service cannot be performed.

A plenary no contact or order of protection could be entered by default for the remedy sought in the petition, if the abuser has been served or given notice in accordance with service requirements and if the abuser then fails to appear as directed or fails to appear on any subsequent appearance or hearing date agreed to by the parties or set by the court. 750 Ill. Comp. Stat. Ann. 60/219(3)-(4) (LexisNexis through P.A. 101-631). It is imperative for the victim to be sure to appear on the necessary court dates in order to move forward with the EOP.

To determine what counties in Illinois offer online access log onto http://www.illinoisprotectionorder.org/OOP/. (Note, this option may not be available in all counties). If available, completing any or all of the initial filing forms online before traveling to the courthouse can save a significant amount of waiting time. Thereafter, the victim will still need to go to the local county courthouse to begin the OP filing process with the Courthouse Clerk. At that time the victim will sign their "Petition for Order of Protection" to attest to its content, and soon thereafter appear in front of a Judge for an Emergency hearing to determine if their Petition for Order of Protection will be granted. If online access to initial OP forms is not available, the victim should travel to the appropriate courthouse to prepare the Petition for Order of Protection and file the OP.

Depending on the county, there are generally court advocates who can assist the victim with the completion of the necessary paperwork. The Court advocates are available to discuss the incidents that caused a victim to seek an OP, as well as discuss what remedies are available for a victim to request from the Judge that may be put in place for the duration of the Emergency OP (14-21 days). 750 Ill. Comp. Stat. Ann. 60/205(b) (LexisNexis through P.A. 101-631). Some of these "remedies" would include, but not be limited to, no physical contact between the victim of the abuser, no contact between the abuser and children of the parties or other family members; no phone or email contact; and exclusive possession of the shared home, if applicable. 750 Ill. Comp. Stat. Ann. 60/214(b)(1), (2), (3) (LexisNexis through P.A. 101-631).

There is also a similar process for filing a Petition requesting a Stalking No Contact Order for eligible persons as mentioned earlier. Similar to filing for an Order of Protection, filing for a Stalking No Contact Order begins with the filing of a petition for a stalking no contact order in any civil court, unless specific courts are designated by local rule or order. 740 Ill. Comp. Stat. Ann. 21/20(a)(1) (LexisNexis through P.A. 101-650). Additionally, an action for a stalking no contact order may be commenced in conjunction with a delinquency petition or a criminal prosecution as provided in Article 112A of the Code of Criminal Procedure of 1963. 740 Ill. Comp. Stat. Ann. 21/20(a)(2). Under Illinois law, no fee is allowed to be charged for filing petitions or modifying or certifying orders in connection with stalking no contact orders. 740 Ill. Comp. Stat. Ann. 21/20(c) (LexisNexis through P.A. 101-650). Similar to an Order of Protection, a petition for a Stalking No Contact Order should be filed in the county where: (1) the petitioner resides, (2) the respondent resides, or (3) one or more of the acts of the alleged stalking has occurred. 740 Ill. Comp. Stat. Ann. 20/55 (LexisNexis through P.A. 101-650).

If granted, an Emergency Stalking No Contact Order shall be effective for no less than 14 days, and no more than 21 days unless it is re-opened or extended or voided by entry or an order of greater duration. 740 Ill. Comp. Stat. Ann. 21/105(a) (LexisNexis through P.A. 101-650). A plenary Stalking No Contact order is effective for a fixed period of time, not to exceed 2 years (unless it is entered in connection with a criminal prosecution or delinquency petition, then the order shall remain in effect as provided in Section 112A-20 of the Code of Criminal Procedure. 740 Ill. Comp. Stat. Ann. 21/105(b) (LexisNexis through PA. 101-650).

The Remedies in an Order of Protection

There are several remedies afforded to victims of domestic violence. Such remedies include an Order of Protection (Emergency and Plenary), a Sexual Assault No Contact Order, and a Stalking No Contact Order. A variety of additional remedy options are available within the order of protection. These remedies vary depending on the circumstances of each case and the Court's discretion to grant remedies for the safety of the petitioner and other protected individuals.

Further IDVA allows for the Judge, at his or her discretion and based on the case facts, to prohibit abuser from continuing threats and abuse (abuse includes physical abuse, harassment, intimidation, interference with personal liberty, or willful deprivation); prohibit abuser from contacting victim through third parties; bar abuser from entering a shared residence, school, work, or other specific location; prohibit the abuser from using drugs or alcohol; and require the abuser to attend certain counseling classes for a period of time. 750 Ill. Comp. Stat. Ann. 60/214(b)(1), (2), (3), and (4) (LexisNexis through P.A. 101-631).

Further remedies in an Order of Protection are to prohibit the concealment or removal of a child out of state, entry of an order returning the child to the Court and setting a restriction or specific visitation rights. 750 Ill. Comp. Stat. Ann. 60/214(b)(5), (6), (7), and (8) (LexisNexis through P.A. 101-631).

Especially in cases where abuse occurred to a minor child, the Judge could bar the abuser's access to any of the child's medical and/or school records. 750 Ill. Comp. Stat. Ann. 60/214(b)(15) (LexisNexis through P.A. 101-631). It is not uncommon for the Illinois court to order temporary physical possession of children while the order of protection is pending. 750 Ill. Comp. Stat. Ann. 70/213(b)(5) (LexisNexis through P.A. 101-631).

It is the Court's duty to be sure to maintain the best interest, safety, and care of the child(ren) involved. In considering the restrictions between the abuser parent and the child(ren), the court will consider the facts presented in the Petition for Order of Protection to determine whether the children need to be a protected party and to what extent protections should be put in place.

If you are obtaining an order of protection from the abuser and personal property has been removed or should be protected, the Order can grant you certain personal property and require the abuser to turn over any of your personal property in their possession. 750 Ill. Comp. Stat. Ann. 60/214(10)-(11) (LexisNexis through P.A. 101-631). Additionally, there is a restriction and language in the Order that will bar the abuser from damaging, destroying, interfering with, or selling certain personal property. 750 Ill. Comp. Stat. Ann. 60/214(11) (LexisNexis through P.A. 101-631).

If you have a concern regarding your personal property, please be sure to provide as many details as possible as to the personal property and the reasons why these items need to be protected in the Petition for Order of Protection.

A Judge could order a temporary allocation of parental responsibilities with respect to significant decision-making on behalf of the minor children. 750 Ill. Comp. Stat. Ann. 60/214(6) (LexisNexis through P.A. 101-631).

The Petitioner could be awarded temporary decision-making responsibility in accordance with this Section, the Illinois Marriage and Dissolution of Marriage Act, the Illinois Parentage Act of 2015 (IMDMA), and the Illinois State's Uniform Child-Custody Jurisdiction and Enforcement Act with respect to education, medical, extracurricular, and religious decision for the child(ren). *Id.* If a court finds, after a hearing, that the abuser has committed abuse of a minor child, there is a rebuttable presumption that awarding temporary significant decision-making responsibility to the abuser would not be in the child's best interest. *Id.*

The court shall restrict or deny an abuser's parenting time with a minor child if the court finds that Respondent (abuser) has done or is likely to do any of the following: (i) abuse or endanger the minor child during parenting time; (ii) use the parenting time as an opportunity to abuse or harass petitioner or petitioner's family or household members; (iii) improperly conceal or detain the minor child; or (iv) otherwise act in a manner that is not in the best interests of the minor child. 750 Ill. Comp. Stat. Ann. 60/214(7) (LexisNexis through P.A. 101-631).

The IDVA provides specifically that the court shall not be limited by the standards set forth in Section 603.10 of the Illinois Marriage and Dissolution of Marriage Act. *Id.* If the court hearing the order of protection grants parenting time for the Respondent, the order must specify dates and times for the parenting time to take place and any other specific parameters or conditions that are appropriate in order for Respondent's parenting time to go forward. *Id.* The order of protection cannot order for parenting time to occur as "reasonable parenting time". *Id.* There must be specificity to the order regarding parenting time. *Id.*

Even while the OP or other protection orders are in place, the abuser can be ordered to pay support for minor child(ren) living with you, for your or your children's shelter or counseling services, and any other expenses that the court deems necessary. 750 Ill. Comp. Stat. Ann. 60/214(12), (16) (LexisNexis through P.A. 101-631). There is a common misconception in Illinois that parenting time is linked to child support. This is a misplaced idea.

Whether you are exercising parenting time or not, your obligation to pay child support does not terminate based on how often you get to spend time with your child.

Think of it this way, whether your child has parenting time with you or not, the child still needs food, medications, shelter, and clothing.

An Immediate "Stay Away" Order will require the respondent to refrain from both physical and non-physical contact with the petitioner. 750 Ill. Comp. Stat. Ann. 60/214(3) (LexisNexis through P.A. 101-631).

This contact can be direct, indirect (including, but not limited to, telephone calls, mail, email, faxes, and written notes), or through third parties who may or may not know about the Order of Protection. The Stay Away Order can also prohibit contact with the minor child/children. If a "Stay Away" Order is not implemented, the Court can enter an order for no offensive contact.

If you have a house or rental property in common with the respondent, the court can order the respondent to leave the residence. 750 Ill. Comp. Stat. Ann. 60/214(2) (LexisNexis through P.A. 101-631). The petitioner can be granted exclusive possession of the residence. *Id.* The respondent will also be prohibited from entering or remaining anywhere while petitioner and/or protected person(s) is/are present. 750 Ill. Comp. Stat. Ann. 60/214(3) (LexisNexis through P.A. 101-631). This measure is to ensure that the abuser will not be present in the same home with the victim to increase the potential of repeat acts of violence.

Within the Order of Protection, the Court has the authority to prohibit the respondent from possessing firearms. 750 Ill. Comp. Stat. Ann. 60/214(14.5)(a) (LexisNexis through P.A. 101-631). Prohibition of firearms possession, pursuant to Section 60/214(14.5), requires that the respondent has received certain due process rights before the respondent is stripped of access to firearms. 750 Ill. Comp. Stat. Ann. 60/214(14.5)(a)(1)-(3) (LexisNexis through P.A. 101-631).

The order of protection must have been issued after a hearing was conducted and the respondent received actual notice and the opportunity to participate. 750 Ill. Comp. Stat. Ann. 60/214(14.5)(a)(1) (LexisNexis through P.A. 101-631). The order of protection must also prohibit and restrain the Respondent from harassing, stalking, threatening and intimidating a partner or child, or engaging in conduct that would place the protected party in reasonable fear of bodily harm to the protected party or child. 750 Ill. Comp. Stat. Ann. 60/214(14.5)(a)(2) (LexisNexis through P.A. 101-631).

Finally, the order of protection must include a finding that the respondent is a credible threat to the physical safety of the protected parties/party. 750 Ill. Comp. Stat. Ann. 60/214(14.5)(a)(3)(i) (LexisNexis through P.A. 101-631). Once the above criteria have been met, then the Respondent will be ordered to turnover firearms and will be prohibited from possessing firearms as long as the order of protection remains in place. 750 Ill. Comp. Stat. Ann. 60/214(a) (LexisNexis through P.A. 101-631).

The Court will issue a warrant for the firearms in possession of the Respondent and the firearms will be held in safekeeping for the duration of the order of protection. 750 Ill. Comp. Stat. Ann. 60/214(14.5)(a)(3)(i) (LexisNexis through P.A. 101-631).

The Respondent's Firearm Owner's Identification Card ("FOID Card") will also be turned over to the local law enforcement agency. *Id.* The respondent cannot buy new firearms. Federal law further prohibits a person who is the subject of an order of protection from possessing a firearm or ammunition that has gone through interstate or foreign commerce. 18 U.S.C.S. § 922(g)(8) (LexisNexis through P.L. 116-145).

In reviewing the matter and deciding the remedies to outline in an EOP, the Judge must balance the hardships of the abuser if the court were to enter a certain remedy. 750 Ill. Comp. Stat. Ann. 60/214(d) (LexisNexis through P.A. 101-631). For example, what will be the hardship on the abuser if he/she was ordered to stay away from their employment and you both work for the same employer?

If the abuser is ordered to pay support and to make financial contributions, interference with either parties' ability to work for an extended period of time could result in a hardship.

The IDVA states that if the court finds that the balance of hardships does not support the granting of certain remedies, which may require such balancing, the court's findings shall so indicate and shall include a finding as to whether granting the remedy will result in hardship to respondent that would substantially outweigh the hardship to petitioner from denial of the remedy. *Id.* The findings shall be an official recording or in writing. *Id.*

A Stalking No Contact Order will order one or more of the following remedies: prohibit the respondent from threatening to commit or committing stalking; order the respondent not to have any contact with the petitioner or a third person specifically named by the court; prohibit the respondent from knowingly coming within, or knowingly remaining within a specified distance of the petitioner or the petitioner's residence, school, daycare, or place of employment, or any specified place frequented by the petitioner; however, the court may order the respondent to stay away from the respondent's own residence, school, or place of employment only if the respondent has been provided actual notice of the opportunity to appear and be heard on the petition; prohibit the respondent from possessing a Firearm Owners Identification Card, or possessing or buying firearms; and order other injunctive relief the court determines to be necessary to protect the petitioner or third party specifically named by the court. 750 Ill. Comp. Stat. Ann. 21/80(b)(1)-(5) (LexisNexis through P.A. 101-631).

The Remedies in a Stalking No Contact Order

If a court finds that the Petitioner has been a victim of stalking, then a stalking no contact order shall issue so long as requirements are met for either an emergency or plenary order. 740 Ill. Comp. Stat. Ann. 21/80(a) (LexisNexis through P.A. 101-650). There are a number of remedies that may be granted in connection with a stalking no contact order, which includes one or more of the following:

1. *Prohibiting the respondent from threatening to commit or committing stalking;*
2. *Order the respondent not to have any contact with the petitioner or a third person specifically named by the court;*
3. *Prohibit the respondent from knowingly coming within, or knowingly remaining within a specified place frequented by the petitioner; however, the court may order the respondent to stay away from the respondent's own residence, school, or place of employment only if the respondent has been provided actual notice of the opportunity to appear and be heard on the petition;*
4. *Prohibit the respondent from possessing a Firearm Owner's Identification Card, or possessing or buying firearms; and*
5. *Order other injunctive relief the court determines to be necessary to protect the petitioner or third party specifically named by the court.*

740 Ill. Comp. Stat. Ann. 21/80(b)(1)-(5) (LexisNexis through P.A. 101-650).

If the respondent of a Stalking No Contact Order is a minor, then there are additional remedies that may be had. If both a protected party and respondent of a Stalking No Contact Order attend the same public, private, or non-public elementary, middle, or high school, then the Court must consider the following: the severity of the act; any continuing physical danger or emotional distress to the petitioner; the educational rights guaranteed to the petitioner and respondent under federal and state law; the availability of a transfer of the respondent to another school, a change of placement or program of the respondent; the expense, difficulty, and educational disruption that would be caused by a transfer of the respondent to another school; and any other relevant facts of the case. 740 Ill. Comp. Stat. Ann. 21/80(b-5) (LexisNexis through P.A. 101-650). The following may be ordered if both a protected party and respondent attend the same public, private, or non-public elementary, middle, or high school: that the respondent not attend the public, private, or non-public elementary, middle or high school attended by the petitioner; that the respondent accept a change or placement or program, as determined by the school district or private or non-public school; or place restrictions on the respondent's movements within the school attended by the petitioner. *Id.* Additionally, if the respondent is a minor, then the Court may order the parents, guardian, or legal custodian to take certain actions or to refrain from taking certain actions, in order to ensure the minor respondent complies with the order. 740 Ill. Comp. Stat. Ann. 21/80(b-6) (LexisNexis through P.A. 101-650).

If a Stalking No Contact Order is granted, the Court may award the petitioner costs and attorney fees. 740 Ill. Comp. Stat. Ann. 21/80(c) (LexisNexis through P.A. 161-650). However, monetary damages are not recoverable as a remedy. 740 Ill. Comp. Stat. Ann. 21/80(d). If the order prohibits the respondent from possessing a Firearm Owner's Identification Card, or possessing or buying firearms, then the Court shall confiscate the respondent's Firearm Owner's Identification Card and immediately return the card to the Department of State Police Firearm Owner's Identification Card Office. 740 Ill. Comp. Stat. Ann. 21/80(e) (LexisNexis through P.A. 161-650).

If a respondent violates a stalking no contact order, the first initial knowing violation of same is a Class A misdemeanor. 740 Ill. Comp. Stat. Ann. 21/125 (LexisNexis through P.A. 101-650). Second or subsequent violates are a Class 4 felony. *Id.* The Stalking No Contact Order must include language advising a respondent of this information. 740 Ill. Comp. Stat. Ann. 21/110 (LexisNexis through P.A. 101-650).

Enforcement of the Order of Protection

Once an Order of Protection is entered, questions may arise regarding the enforcement of the order. What happens if the abuser violates the order? Violation of an order of protection can lead to criminal or civil sanctions. If the accuser is in violation, call the police or the sheriff. Even if you think it is a minor violation, call the police to help enforce the order and to make sure you are safe. An Order of Protection is only a piece of paper unless the petitioner enforces the order.

The Illinois Domestic Violence Act requires the police to take all reasonable steps in preventing further abuse. 750 Ill. Comp. Stat. Ann. 60/304(a) (LexisNexis through P.A. 101-631). If police are called, be sure to write down the name(s) of the responding officers and their badge number(s) just in case you may need to follow up at a later date. Insist that a police report is filed, even if no arrest is made. Have a copy of the order of protection ready to show the police. You should keep a copy of the order of protection at home, at your office, and on your person at all times. If the police do not arrest the Respondent or file a criminal complaint, there is still the option to file for civil contempt for a violation of the order. 750 Ill. Comp. Stat. Ann. 60/223(b) (LexisNexis through P.A. 101-631). It is a crime and contempt of court if the abuser knowingly violates the order in any way.

Once a respondent receives service of an Emergency Order of Protection (EOP), he/she must abide by it. Even if the order was obtained by false testimony, resist the urge to correct the wrong by confronting the accuser. Do not use third parties to communicate for you while the EOP or any order of protection is in place. Violating the EOP or any order of protection may result in prosecution for contempt of court or violation of an Order of Protection. The violation would be a Class A Misdemeanor, which is punishable by 364 days incarceration sentence and or up to $2,500.00 in fines. 720 Ill. Comp. Stat. Ann. 5/12-3.4(d) (LexisNexis through P.A. 101-631); 730 Ill. Comp. Stat. Ann. 5/5-4.5-55(a), (e) (LexisNexis through P.A. 101-631). The violation will likely result in a Plenary Order of Protection being granted or extended.

If an Order of Protection has been filed against you, you will need to prepare your defense. One method is to dispute the allegations with presentation of evidence to refute the claims against you. Be prepared to present witnesses that were present when the alleged incident(s) took place and find someone who could testify that no threatening conduct occurred.

Physical evidence, such as pictures, receipts or phone records or logs may also help contradict the plaintiff's assertion that there was threatening behavior. You may subpoena any records you deem necessary and compel the attendance of any necessary or material witnesses. Typically, a hearing for a Plenary Order of Protection will be assigned to a large court docket that can take a few hours to get through. Contact your witnesses prior to the court date and be sure that they will be present in court on the day of the hearing.

Bring any physical evidence with you to court. Some counties may prohibit camera phones from entering the building. If you have evidence on your camera phone, you may ask the clerk when checking in to grant an order allowing you to bring the cell phone into the building. If an order of protection is filed and there are impending divorce proceedings, then it is likely that your divorce matter and order of protection will be combined or heard by the same Judge.

Seeking help for victims of Domestic Violence is essential to the victim's survival and the process of regaining a sense of self. The longer abuse continues there is more potential long term physical and psychological damage the victim possibly will experience.

There are many avenues for victims to seek help, and some are provided below:

- If you are hurt or in impending danger, please call **911** immediately and do whatever you can to get into a safer situation.
- Consider seeking an Order of Protection.
- Contact an attorney for support within the judicial system and to understand your legal rights in a Domestic Violence situation.
- Contact the **National Domestic Violence Hotline at 800-799-SAFE (7233) or 800-787-3224 (TDD**). The national hotline can guide you to local shelters in your community and/or to vital services.
- Seek local therapists and counselors to provide support through the healing process.

Help does exist for Victims who experience Domestic Violence; and an understanding of the options available is a key component to providing the victim with the specific help that they need.

Karina's Law: New Provisions to Protect Survivors of Domestic Violence in Illinois

Effective May 11, 2025, Illinois' **Karina's Law** is in force as a new piece of legislation aimed at strengthening protections for survivors of domestic violence. Named in honor of Karina Gonzalez, the law was enacted to close dangerous gaps in the enforcement of firearm restrictions tied to orders of protection.

Karina and her 15-year-old daughter, Daniela, were tragically killed in 2023 by Karina's estranged husband, who still had access to guns despite a court-issued order of protection. Karina's story is heartbreaking, but her legacy is now shaping the future of domestic violence response in Illinois.

What Karina's Law Does

Karina's Law (HB4144) enhances the ability of courts and law enforcement to remove firearms from individuals who pose a threat in domestic violence situations. Key provisions include:

- **Mandatory Firearm Surrender**

  Individuals subject to an order of protection must surrender all firearms, and any parts that can be assembled into operable weapons, within **24 hours** of being served. (Illinois General Assembly, 2024)

- **Search Warrants for Firearm Seizure**

  Judges are now authorized to issue **search-and-seizure warrants** when there is probable cause that a respondent still has access to weapons and poses an immediate threat to the petitioner.

- **Clearer Law Enforcement Procedures**

  The law outlines responsibilities for law enforcement agencies to ensure the **timely removal, documentation, and safekeeping** of surrendered or seized firearms.

These changes address the most vulnerable period for survivors, immediately after filing for an emergency order of protection, when retaliation by an abuser can escalate dangerously.

Larger Context

From 2019 to 2023, Illinois experienced a 63% increase in domestic violence-related gun deaths. Advocates emphasize that the most dangerous time for victims is immediately after legal action is taken, when firearm removal can be the difference between life and death.

Karina's law responds to this crisis, empowering courts and law enforcement with clearer authority and faster timelines to act.

LEGAL DISCLAIMER

The content of this publication has been prepared by Gwendolyn J. Sterk and the Family Law Group, P.C., for informational purposes only, and does not constitute legal advice, nor does it create or constitute an attorney-client relationship.

You should contact an attorney for individual advice regarding your specific situation. Do not send us information until you speak with one of our attorneys and secure authorization to send that information to us. We cannot represent you until we know our representation of you will not result in a conflict of interest and an agreement is reached between you and us as to the terms of your engagement with our firm. **This book was created to provide general information only.**

This book may include links or references providing direct access to other resources including websites. Gwendolyn J. Sterk and the Family Law Group, P.C. is not responsible for the accuracy or content of information contained in these outside sources. Links, articles or references from Gwendolyn J. Sterk and the Family Law Group, P.C. to third-party sites or providers **do not constitute an endorsement by Gwendolyn J. Sterk and the Family Law Group, P.C. of the parties or their products and services.**

Gwendolyn J. Sterk and the Family Law Group, P.C. has been granted Limited Licensing for stock images. All images and other content in this publication (collectively the "Content"), as well as the selection and arrangement of the Content, are protected by copyright, trademark, patent, trade secret and other intellectual property laws and treaties (collectively, "Intellectual Property Laws"). Any unauthorized use of any Content may violate such laws and the Terms of Use.

Gwendolyn J. Sterk and the Family Law Group, P.C. does not grant any express or implied permission to use any Content. You agree not to copy, republish, frame, link to, download, transmit, modify, adapt, create derivative works based on, rent, lease, loan, sell, assign, distribute, display, perform, license, sublicense or reverse engineer the site or any or the content. All Images in this book are protected by United States and international copyright laws and treaties.

Empower Yourself With Order of Protection Forms

Approved Statewide Forms - Order of Protection
https://www.illinoiscourts.gov/
[Approved May 2025]

If you presently reside in the State of Illinois...empower yourself to stop domestic violence by submitting the approved statewide *Order of Protection Forms* online via e-File, postal mail or in-person at the Circuit Court Clerk's Office.

To ensure you have everything you will need beforehand, the next section of this book provides physical copies of the exact forms found online. These forms possess the power to give you back your life.

Empower yourself by reading through the forms, as many times as you need, making notes, gathering the information you will need, and penciling in your answers in this book, so you can quickly and easily copy the required information over to the final forms when you are ready to submit.

The forthcoming pages include *How to Ask for an Order of Protection, Petition for Order of Protection, Additional Incidents of Abuse, Additional Case Information, Confidential Name & Location of the School or Daycare, Affidavit of Parenting Time Supervisor, Emergency Order of Protection, Order of Protection, Summons (Protective Orders), Proof of Service of Summons and Warrant for Seizure of Fire Arms.*

While it is perfectly acceptable to submit the *Order of Protection Forms* yourself, it is strongly advised to seek legal counsel from the licensed attorney of your choice, or Illinois Legal Aid Online at https://www.illinoislegalaid.org/legal-information/order-protection. Empower yourself with every option and legal remedy available by reaching out to caring professionals for help.

illinoiscourts.gov/documents-and-forms/approved-forms/circuit-courtstandardized-forms-suites/order-of-protection/

HOW TO ASK FOR AN ORDER OF PROTECTION

1 PETITIONER FILLS OUT FORMS AND STARTS A CASE.

To start an Order of Protection, you (the Petitioner) begin by filling out a *Petition for Order of Protection*. The *Petition* tells the judge why you believe you need an Order of Protection. Write down everything that has been happening and why you need the order. You may be able to work with an advocate to prepare this paperwork and go to court (call the Illinois Statewide Domestic Violence Hotline at 877-863-6338).

Use this form:
○ *Petition for Order of Protection*

2 A JUDGE HEARS YOUR PETITION.

The judge will look over the forms you submitted and ask you any questions. If you asked for an *Emergency Order of Protection* and the judge thinks it's needed, the judge will issue a temporary order called an *Emergency Order of Protection*. This temporary order is a short-term measure to keep you safe until a more in-depth hearing can happen with both sides.

Use this form:
○ *Emergency Order of Protection*

3 NOTICE TO THE OTHER PERSON.

The Respondent will receive a copy of all the paperwork. This is typically done by the sheriff in your county. Sometimes it can take the sheriff a few tries before they are able to find and notify the Respondent.

Use this form:
○ *Summons (Protective Orders)*

4 ATTEND THE COURT HEARING.

After the Respondent has been notified about the order, both sides will attend a final hearing in court. This is the opportunity to present your case in more detail. Bring any evidence, documents, or witnesses that support your need for protection. The judge will carefully consider the information presented and decide whether a long-term order, known as the *Order of Protection*, is necessary.

Use this form:
○ *Order of Protection*

Laws covering these forms: 750 Illinois Compiled Statutes, section 60/101 through section 60/401 and 725 ILCS 5/112A.

This overview is not legal advice. It provides general instructions on how to use these forms in your court case. It cannot and does not try to cover everything that might happen in your court case. Your use of the forms does not guarantee you will be successful in court.

How a judge handles a case can vary from county to county. **Your county may have special requirements that are not covered in these instructions.** Ask the Circuit Clerk if your county has local rules and, if so, where you can get a copy.

STEP 1

FILL OUT AND FILE FORMS. START YOUR CASE.

ARE THESE FORMS FOR ME?

You may **use these forms to ask the court for an Order of Protection** when:
- ○ you have been abused by a family or household member, caregiver, current or ex-romantic partner, or current or ex-spouse, a person with whom you live or used to live, or someone who is the other parent of your child; or
- ○ you are filing on behalf of any person who has been abused by a family or household member, but is unable to file on their own.

Who else can be protected by my Order of Protection?
- ▪ Anyone who lives or works in your house;
- ▪ Your minor children, even if they don't live with you; and
- ▪ High risk adults with disabilities.

If none of the above relationships exist, do not use these forms. You may be eligible for a different type of protective order.
- ▪ Stalking: illinoislegalaid.org/stalkingnocontact
- ▪ Sexual Assault: illinoislegalaid.org/civilnocontact

Forms You Will Need to Complete
- ○ *Petition for Order of Protection*: gives the court information to decide if you can get an *Order of Protection*.
- ○ *Emergency Order of Protection* (if requesting an EOP): a proposed order that will be reviewed by the judge during your court hearing without letting the Respondent know. The judge may make changes to the Order after you present your case. The Order will either be granted or denied.
- ○ *Order of Protection:* a proposed long-term Order, commonly called a plenary order. This will be reviewed by the judge during your court hearing. The judge may make changes to the Order after you present your case. The Order will either be granted or denied.
- ○ *Summons (Protective Orders)*: tells the Respondent that you have asked for an *Order of Protection* against them.

Information you will need to complete the forms:
- ○ Description of current and past abuse;
- ○ Names of other people to be protected;
- ○ Addresses and property you want protected;
- ○ Name and date of birth of the Respondent, if known;
- ○ Addresses where the Respondent can be found, if known.

You May Also Need These Forms
- ○ *Letter to the Sheriff*: asks the sheriff to deliver the *Summons* to the Respondent.
- ○ *Confidential Name & Location of the School or Daycare* (if needed): use this if you do not want the Respondent to know about addresses of schools or daycares in your Petition.
- ○ *Affidavit of Parenting Time Supervisor* (if needed): this needs to be signed by the person who has agreed to be responsible and supervise the Respondent's parenting time.

Where can I get the forms?
- ○ You can get printed forms from the Circuit Clerk at your local courthouse. You can find the forms online at: ilcourts.info/forms.
- ○ You can also use an Easy Form. Learn more about that on page 4.

Will I have to pay to file an Order of Protection and notify the Respondent?
- ○ No. Filing an Order of Protection case and delivery by the Sheriff to Respondent is free.

What is the difference between an *Emergency Order of Protection (EOP)* and an *Order of Protection (OP)?*

	Emergency Order of Protection	Order of Protection
When would the order take effect?	An *Emergency Order of Protection* takes effect **after you appear before the judge and the judge signs the Order.** Your hearing for the EOP may happen immediately after filing the *Petition*.	An *Order of Protection* takes effect **after the Respondent gets notice** and after a court hearing. Unless you are granted an *Emergency Order of Protection*, you will not have an Order of Protection until after that hearing.
How long will the protective order last?	Civil case: the EOP lasts for **14 to 21 days** until there is a hearing on the long-term order. Criminal case: the EOP lasts **until the request** for a final OP can be heard.	Civil case: may last for **up to 2 years**. Criminal case: may last for the **duration of the prosecution and/or up to 2 years** past the end of any criminal sentence.
Is the Respondent notified before the hearing?	The law **does not require Respondent to know** before the emergency hearing.	Civil case: the **sheriff notifies** the Respondent and a hearing with both the Petitioner and the Respondent takes place. Criminal case: the OP may be issued at any court date where the **defendant is present or after they are notified.**
When does the court hearing take place?	The court hearing for an EOP may happen **immediately** after filing your Petition. Ask the clerk for directions to the courtroom or instructions on how to participate in court.	A **future court date** may be set for you by the clerk to come back and ask for your Order.

Where can I file the forms?

- File your forms with the Clerk of the Circuit Court in the county where:
  - you live; or
  - Respondent lives; or
  - the abuse occurred; or
  - you are staying to avoid abuse.
- After you file your forms, the clerk will give you a hearing date.

Make sure you know how to attend your court date.
Your court date could be in person, by phone, or by video. If it is by phone or video, it is called a "Remote Appearance." Call the Circuit Clerk or visit their website for more information. To find the phone number for your Circuit Clerk, visit ilcourts.info/clerks.

Firearms and Orders of Protection

If you are asking the court for an Order of Protection, you can also ask the judge for "firearms relief" in Section 14.5 of your petition.

Before you ask for this, it's important to understand what firearms relief means so you can decide what's safest and best for you.

What is firearms relief?
There are two types of firearms relief a judge can order:

1. **Surrender of Firearms**
   The judge can order the Respondent to give up any firearms, firearm parts, and their Firearm Owner's Identification (FOID) card to law enforcement.

2. **Search Warrant**
   The judge can allow law enforcement to enter and search a place—like a home, vehicle, garage, or storage unit—to take firearms, firearm parts, or the FOID card.

How It Works

Surrender Order	Search Warrant
o The judge may issue just a surrender order or both a surrender order and a search warrant. o The Respondent must give any firearms they have with them to law enforcement when served. o The Respondent has 24 hours after being served to give law enforcement any firearms stored elsewhere. o Law enforcement will report back to the court about what is surrendered.	o If the judge issues a search warrant, they will also issue a surrender order. o It may take law enforcement up to 10 days to carry out the search. o You will be notified if anything changes with the warrant. o Law enforcement can only take firearms found in the location listed in the warrant. o You will be asked to fill out an information sheet to help with the search. This sheet is not confidential. o Law enforcement must report to the court anything taken during the search.

Note: If you are asking for a **criminal** Order of Protection, only law enforcement or the State's Attorney's Office can request a search warrant. You can talk to the police department handling your case or ask the State's Attorney for help.

Need More Help?
If you're not sure whether to ask for firearms relief, or if you want help finding a shelter or talking to a domestic violence advocate, **call the Illinois Domestic Violence Hotline at 877-863-6338.** Help is free and confidential.

Frequently Asked Questions:
Firearms and Orders of Protection

Do I have to ask for firearms to be taken away from the Respondent?
No. It's your choice. You can ask for a search warrant or surrender of firearms. If asking for a search warrant or surrender of firearms doesn't feel safe or right for you, you don't have to include it in your petition.

What do I need to ask for a search warrant?
You'll need to give specific information about why the Respondent having firearms is a threat to you. You'll also need to describe where the firearms are kept (such as the address, or a description of the vehicle). If a search warrant is granted, you will provide more details to law enforcement to help them carry it out.

The judge will need to know:
1. Does the Respondent pose a credible threat to your physical safety?
2. Does the Respondent have firearms or firearm parts that could be assembled to make an operable firearm in their possession?
3. Where are those firearms or firearm parts located?

What happens if the police find something illegal during a search?
If police see something illegal, they can take action, including arresting the person who owns the illegal items.

What if the firearms aren't legally owned by the Respondent?
The judge can still order the firearms to be taken. However, the Respondent—or whoever owns them—could face criminal charges.

Will the Order of Protection and the search warrant be served at the same time?
Not always. Law enforcement is encouraged to serve both at the same time if possible, but it may not happen that way.

Will the Respondent know there's a search warrant?
Maybe. The Respondent might find out when they are served with the Order of Protection. **If you're concerned that the Respondent finding out about the warrant could impact your safety, you can call the Illinois Domestic Violence Hotline at 877-863-6338 for support and resources.**

Can firearms be given to someone else instead of the police?
No, unless the judge allows it. If the judge orders the surrender of firearms, the Respondent must give their firearms to the police. Later, the judge may allow the firearms to be transferred to someone else. If that happens, you'll be told and given a chance to share any concerns with the court.

Will the Respondent get the firearms back?
Possibly. When the Order of Protection ends, the Respondent can request their firearms back—if they have a valid FOID card.

EXTRA HELP WITH THE FORMS

What if I need help filling out my forms?

- ○ Advocates may be available to assist you. If you want to speak with an advocate, call the Illinois Statewide Domestic Violence Hotline at 877-863-6338.
- ○ If you need help with the writing or filing of the *Petition*, ask the Circuit Clerk for assistance.
- ○ If you are requesting an Order of Protection after an incident of abuse where the Respondent was arrested or charged with a crime, you may be able to ask your County's State's Attorney's Office for assistance.
- ○ You may also ask someone to assist you in filling out the forms.

Easy Form

Illinois Legal Aid Online has an Easy Form program that helps you complete your forms. Easy Forms ask simple questions and put your answers in the right places on the forms. At the end of the program, you can download or email your forms to e-file or print them.

Easy Forms are free to use. Visit ilao.info/op-easy-form or scan the QR code to use the Easy Form.

IL Court Help

For more information about going to court including how to fill out and file forms, call or text **Illinois Court Help** at 833-411-1121 or go to ilcourthelp.gov.

If there are any words or terms used in these instructions that you do not understand, please **visit Illinois Legal Aid Online** at ilao.info/glossary. You may also find more information, resources, and the location of your local legal self-help center at ilao.info/lshc-directory.

ILAO
ILLINOIS LEGAL AID ONLINE

COSTS AND FEES

There may be costs and fees to take part in a court case. These fees and costs can include fees for filing court documents and Sheriff's fees for providing notice. Depending on the type of court case, there may be other costs and fees charged. If you cannot afford to pay costs and fees, you can ask the court to file for free or at a reduced cost by filing an *Application for Waiver of Court Fees*.

This is a separate form you can find at: ilcourts.info/fee-waiver-forms.

HOW TO FILE THE FORMS

Note: You do not have to e-file in Order of Protection cases.

Not E-filing

- Some people are not required to e-file, which means they can file paper forms at the courthouse or by mail. People who do not have to e-file are:
    - Inmates in prison or jail who do not have a lawyer.
    - People with a disability that keeps them from e-filing.
- You may also qualify for an exemption from e-filing if you:
    - Do not have internet or computer access in your home, and it is hard for you to travel.
    - Have trouble reading, writing, or speaking English.
    - Are filing documents in a sensitive case, such as an order of protection.
    - Tried to e-file your forms, but you were not able to because the equipment or help you needed was not available.
- To ask for an exemption from e-filing, use the form at ilcourts.info/exempt. If you cannot print this form, then ask for it at your local courthouse.
    - File your *Certification for Exemption from E-Filing* form along with your other court forms at the Circuit Clerk's office or by mail.
    - Bring or send your signed court forms and at least two copies of your forms to the Circuit Clerk's office. Ask them to stamp your copies and return them to you.
    - If you need to make copies of your forms, you can do that at the Circuit Clerk's office. They may charge you a fee to make copies.
- There may be fees to file your forms. See the previous Costs & Fees page for more information. If you mail your court forms to the Circuit Clerk's office, include a stamped envelope addressed to you. The Circuit Clerk will file your forms and then send your copies back to you in the envelope.

E-filing

- After you fill out your court forms, file them with the Circuit Clerk. This is done by electronic filing, called 'e-filing'. You do not have to e-file if:
    - You qualify for an exemption (see "Not E-filing" below) or
    - Your case involves a criminal matter.
- Most people e-file their forms using Odyssey eFileIL at ilcourts.info/efile.
- There may be fees to file your forms. See the previous Costs & Fees page for more information.
- Follow step-by-step instructions and watch videos that walk you through the steps for e-filing at ilcourts.info/efile-info.
- E-filing is easier on a computer. It may not work on a cell phone or tablet.
- If you do not have access to a computer or if you need help e-filing, take your completed forms to a public library or a Circuit Clerk, Appellate Clerk, or Supreme Court Clerks' office. These places offer public computers where you can e-file your forms.
    - Depending on your courthouse, you can bring your forms on paper and there may be public computers with a scanner where you can turn your paper forms into electronic files.
    - Librarians and courthouse staff may be able to help you e-file, but they cannot provide legal advice.

WHAT'S NEXT

STEP 2

A JUDGE HEARS YOUR PETITION.

o If you are asking for an *Emergency Order of Protection*, you need to attend a court hearing.
  ▪ Your hearing for an *Emergency Order of Protection* may happen immediately after filing.
  ▪ If you are not requesting an *Emergency Order of Protection*, skip to step 3.

Will a decision be made at my hearing?

o The judge has to make a decision. The decision is called a court order.
o After the hearing, the judge will either grant or deny your request.
  ▪ **If granted**, an *Emergency Order of Protection* will be entered and start as soon as the Respondent is notified by law enforcement. You will receive a copy of the *Order*. This *Order* can last up to 21 days. Another court date will be scheduled for a hearing on the *Order of Protection*.
  ▪ **If denied**, you will not get an *Emergency Order of Protection*.
  ▪ If the judge decides there is no emergency, but you may need an Order, they will schedule another court date for a hearing to decide whether you will get an *Order of Protection*. This means that you do not have an *Order of Protection* yet.
  ▪ If you were not granted an *Emergency Order of Protection* and **do not** want the Respondent to be served, you can cancel your *Petition*.

STEP 3

NOTIFY THE OTHER PERSON.

o If the Respondent lives in Illinois, the sheriff in the county where the Respondent resides will serve the Respondent with copies of your forms and notice of the court date without charge.
  ▪ If Respondent lives in the same county where the case was filed, the Circuit Clerk will tell you how to get copies of it to the sheriff.
  ▪ If Respondent does not live in the same county where the case was filed call the Sheriff or Circuit Clerk where Respondent lives to find out what they need to serve the Respondent.
o If you receive the *Affidavit of Service*, which is included in the *Summons*, mailed back to you after the Respondent has been served, file it with the Circuit Clerk's office.

What if the sheriff could not deliver the Summons to the Respondent before the hearing?

o The judge may ask if you know a better address where the sheriff can deliver the papers and court notice.
o If you have an *Emergency Order of Protection*, the judge may extend it and give you a court date to return. The sheriff will again try to give notice of the Order to the Respondent.
o If the sheriff can't find the Respondent to deliver the papers, you can ask the judge to allow service by publication in a newspaper.

STEP 4

ATTEND THE COURT HEARING.

Prepare for the Hearing

- Decide what you want to present to the judge.
  - Think about what you will say to the judge if asked to tell your side of the case.
  - Gather and make copies of pictures and documents you want the judge to see, such as receipts, text messages, and photos. Bring the original for the judge and one copy for yourself and Respondent (if present).
- Prepare questions for witnesses. If you want the judge to hear from other people, those people will have to come to court and be witnesses (in most cases, you cannot bring in written statements of witnesses).
- If you have a criminal order, speak to your local State's Attorney's Office.

Go to your Court Hearing

- Bring these items with you to court:
  - Copies of all the documents you filed with the Circuit Clerk; AND
  - Any witnesses and questions you have for them;
  - Other evidence you have to show that your story is true, such as receipts, text messages, and photos.
- Get to the courthouse at least 30 minutes early.
- Go to the courtroom number listed on your court form. If your forms do not have a courtroom number look for a list of cases at the courthouse or ask the Circuit Clerk.
- Check in with the courtroom staff and wait for your name and case number to be called.
- When your case is called, walk to the judge and introduce yourself.
- If your court date is by phone or video:
  - Make sure to have the call-in or login information for your court date and make sure your technology is working.
  - Follow the instructions on the court notice you received. Call the Circuit Clerk or Circuit Court or visit their websites for specific technology instructions.
    - Follow these recommendations to appear by phone or video: ilcourts.info/remote-resources.

Must all parties be present at the court hearing?

- The Petitioner must be in court to get the Order. The Respondent needs to know about the hearing.
  - If Respondent does not come to court, the judge may grant the Petitioner a more long-term *Order of Protection*.
  - If Respondent comes to court, Respondent may agree to an *Order* or may ask for a hearing.
  - The judge can either hold the hearing immediately, or give you or Respondent more time to try to find a lawyer or gather evidence.

How do I present my case to the judge?

- Tell the judge your side of the case and answer questions.
- Use evidence including documents and photos.
  - Give a copy to the judge. Be prepared to explain why the document or photo is important.
- Question witnesses.
  - Tell the judge the name of your witnesses.
  - Ask the witnesses questions you prepared before the hearing.
  - The judge and Respondent may ask questions of you and your witness.

What do I do when Respondent presents their case?

- If present, Respondent will also get to present their case by testifying, giving the judge evidence, and questioning witnesses.
- You will get to see any documents and photos Respondent brings to court. If you do not think the judge should consider them in making a decision about your case, tell the judge why.
- You may ask questions of the Respondent and their witnesses. Write down your questions while they are speaking, so you're ready to ask them during your turn.

What will happen after my hearing?

- The judge has to make a decision. The decision is called a court order.
- After the hearing, the judge will either grant or deny your request.
  - **If granted,** you will be given a copy of the *Order* and it has to be served on Respondent.
    - Read through the *Order* to make sure nothing is wrong or missing.
    - Ask the Circuit Clerk who will give the *Order* to Respondent. If Respondent does not come to court, Respondent must be served with the *Order*. To serve Respondent, follow the instructions under Step 3 above.
    - Always keep a copy of the *Order* with you.
    - Give copies of the *Order* to anyone else who should have it, such as your workplace, child's school, childcare provider, or local police department.
    - If Respondent violates any part of the *Order*, call the police immediately.
  - **If denied,** you will not get an *Order of Protection*.

YOU'VE COMPLETED THE STEPS TO ASK FOR AN ORDER OF PROTECTION.

PETITION FOR
ORDER OF PROTECTION

IN THE STATE OF ILLINOIS, CIRCUIT COURT

☐ **Amended Petition**
Check the box if you already filed a Petition and want to change it.

COUNTY: _____
County Where You Are Filing the Case

Enter the case information as it appears on your other court documents.

PETITIONER: _____
Who started the case.   First, Middle, and Last Name

Filing on behalf of a ☐ minor or ☐ high-risk adult: _____

RESPONDENT: _____
Who you are seeking protection from.   First, Middle, and Last Name

_____
Case Number

> ❗ If you are completing this form on behalf of a minor child, dependent adult, or high-risk adult, fill out information below as if you were that person. Do not use your information, except as directed at the bottom of page 14 where you will sign this form.

I am asking to protect the following people:

Check the boxes for **all** people you want to include in the *Order* and include their names.

☐ Petitioner: _____

☐ Petitioner's minor children with Respondent:

_____
_____

☐ Petitioner's other minor children:

_____
_____

☐ Dependent adult: _____

☐ High-risk adult: _____

☐ Other household members:

_____
_____

Petitioner fills out:

☐ Civil Petition
Petitioner is requesting this Order of Protection be heard as a **civil matter**, not as a part of any criminal case.

_____
Related Civil Case Number

☐ Criminal Petition
Petitioner is requesting this Order of Protection be heard with a **criminal or delinquency case** against Respondent due to the same incident.

_____
Related Criminal or Delinquency Case Number (if known)

TYPE OF ORDER OF PROTECTION REQUESTED AGAINST RESPONDENT *(check all that apply):*

Check either or both boxes for the type of order you want. If you need protection today, check the first one.

☐ Emergency Order of Protection (civil case) / Ex Parte Protective Order (criminal case)
These short-term Orders of Protection can be granted on the same day you file your Petition without advance written notice to Respondent because advance notice would cause more abuse.

☐ Plenary Order of Protection (civil case) / Final Protective Order (criminal case)
These long-term Orders of Protection can only be granted at a court hearing after advance written notice to Respondent.

This form is approved by the Illinois Supreme Court and must be accepted in all Illinois Courts. Forms are free at ilcourts.info/forms.
ATJ 403.5   Page 1 of 15   (05/25)

31

BACKGROUND INFORMATION

A. Petitioner's address:

☐ Respondent should not know household address because it may cause more abuse. Use this alternative address for Court notices. *(Not Petitioner's household address)*:

_____.
Street, Apt. #   City   State   ZIP

- or -

☐ Respondent already knows or can know household address and it is:

_____.
Street, Apt. #   City   State   ZIP

B. Respondent's Personal Information:

Date of Birth: _____ (put approximate age if date of birth is unknown)

Respondent's home address:

_____
Street, Apt. #   City   State   ZIP

Respondent's work information, including when usually work:

_____   _____
Respondent's Employer Name   Respondent's Work Hours

_____
Respondent's Employer Street Address   City   State   ZIP

Other Respondent identifiers if known:

Gender: _____ Height: _____ Weight: _____

Race: _____ Hair Color: _____ Eye Color: _____

Does the Respondent have any distinguishing features like scars, marks, or tattoos?

_____

C. This *Petition* may be filed in this county because *(check all that apply)*:

☐ Petitioner resides in this county.

☐ Respondent resides in this county.

☐ The abuse happened in this county.

☐ Petitioner fled to this county to avoid abuse.

D. How is Respondent related to Petitioner? *(check all that apply)*

Check all the boxes that describe your relationship to Respondent. For example, if you are requesting an Order of Protection against your mother, you will check the box next to "Child" because you are the child of the Respondent.

☐ Current or past dating relationship (BG)

☐ Have children together; never married (CC)

☐ Has or allegedly has a child together

☐ Related through current or past marriage:
   ☐ Spouse (SE)
   ☐ Ex-Spouse (XS)
   ☐ In-law (IL)
   ☐ Step-Child (SC)
   ☐ Step-Brother / Step-Sister / Step-Sibling (SS)
   ☐ Other Family Member (OF)

☐ Sharing or have shared a home (CS)

☐ Related through blood:
   ☐ Child (CH)
   ☐ Parent (PA)
   ☐ Brother / Sister / Sibling (SB)
   ☐ Grandchild (GC)
   ☐ Grandparent (GP)
   ☐ Other Family Member (OF)

☐ Has a blood relationship through a child

☐ Has a family or household relationship with a child who is the:
   ☐ adoptive, prospective adoptive, or foster child of the Petitioner; or
   ☐ of whom the Petitioner is the legal guardian or custodian

☐ Personal caregiver of the Petitioner, who has disabilities or who otherwise needs care

*Answer Sections **E** and **F** the best you can. If you check 'yes' but do not know some of the information asked for, then write "do not know." If you need more room, check the box, fill out the Additional Case Information form, and file it with this Petition.*

E. Is there now, or has there ever been, another *Order of Protection* entered between Petitioner and Respondent?

☐ Yes ☐ No ☐ Do not know

If yes, list information about the cases:

Names of People Involved	County & State	Year	Case No.	Pending?
				☐ Yes ☐ No
				☐ Yes ☐ No
				☐ Yes ☐ No

☐ I have listed additional case information on the *Additional Case Information* form.

F. Is there now, or has there ever been, another court case between Petitioner and Respondent?

List all other types of court cases that you have been involved in with Respondent, such as divorce, custody, child support, parentage, parenting time, guardianship, adoption, criminal, or abuse and neglect cases.

☐ Yes ☐ No ☐ Do not know

If yes, list information about the cases:

Names of People Involved	County & State	Year	Case No.	Pending?
				☐ Yes ☐ No
				☐ Yes ☐ No
				☐ Yes ☐ No

☐ I have listed additional case information on the *Additional Case Information* form.

G. An *Order of Protection* is needed because Respondent did these things:

It is important to be as detailed as you can, with times and dates if you know them or as close as possible. **Include facts that support or explain whatever protections you are asking for.** *Start with the most recent incident or event that caused you to file this Petition.*

Date: _____ Time: _____ Description of what happened:

_____
_____
_____
_____
_____
_____

Date: _____ Time: _____ Description of what happened:

_____
_____
_____
_____
_____
_____
_____

Date: _____ Time: _____ Description of what happened:

_____
_____
_____
_____
_____
_____
_____

Date: _____ Time: _____ Description of what happened:

_____
_____
_____
_____
_____
_____
_____

☐ I needed more room. I filled out the attached *Additional Incidents of Abuse* form or my own extra pages and filed it with this *Petition*.

PROTECTIONS REQUESTED BY PETITIONER

☐ **1. No Abuse**

Respondent be ordered not to threaten or commit the following acts of abuse towards Petitioner and protected people. (*check all that apply*):

Check each box for the type of abuse you want to prevent. If you are not sure what a word means, you can look at definitions on the last page of this form.

☐ Harassment
☐ Physical Abuse
☐ Stalking
☐ Willful Deprivation

☐ Intimidation of a Dependent
☐ Exploitation of a High-Risk Adult with Disabilities
☐ Neglect of a High-Risk Adult with Disabilities
☐ Interference with Personal Liberty

☐ 2. **Possession of Residence**

These remedies do not affect who owns the property, only who gets to use or occupy it.

a. Petitioner be granted exclusive possession of the residence and Respondent be ordered to stay away or not be at the residence BECAUSE *(check one)*:

☐ Petitioner has a right to occupy the residence and Respondent has no right; or

☐ Petitioner and Respondent both have a right to occupy the residence but it would be harder on Petitioner or any children or dependents of the Petitioner to leave.

b. Petitioner's residence is located at *(check one)*:

If you did not list your address on page 2, check the first box to keep it confidential. Check the second box and enter your address if you listed it on page 2.

☐ Petitioner's address is confidential.

or

☐ _____
      Street, Apt. #   *City*   *State*   *ZIP*

☐ c. Respondent be ordered to provide different housing, and stay away from that alternate housing for Petitioner to live in because the parties share a residence. *(Available only after actual notice to Respondent and/or a hearing with the judge)*

☐ 3. **Stay Away from Petitioner, Protected People, and Certain Places** *(see box below)*

Read the information in the box below and make sure that is what you want. If so, check each box below that applies.

Respondent be ordered to *(check all that apply)*:

☐ a. Stay away from Petitioner and protected people at all times, and not have any contact, including through third parties.

> **IMPORTANT**: If ordered to stay away from Petitioner and protected people, Respondent must not have ANY physical, non-physical, direct, or indirect contact with Petitioner and protected people. This includes oral communication, written communication, sign language, telephone and cell phone calls, faxes, texts, tweets, emails, posts, or communication by any other social media, and all other communication with Petitioner and protected people. This also includes contact or communication through others who may not know about the *Order of Protection.*

☐ b. Not go to or stay at any of the following places while Petitioner is there:

NOTE: *Respondent will see these addresses. If you do not want Respondent to know any of these addresses do not list it and instead check the box below the address line*

☐ Places of employment of Petitioner, located at:

_____   _____
Name   *Street Address*   *City*   *State*   *ZIP*
                                    or ☐ I wish to keep the address confidential

_____   _____
Name   *Street Address*   *City*   *State*   *ZIP*
                                    or ☐ I wish to keep the address confidential

☐ Schools, kindergartens, or daycare centers of Petitioner, located at:

Name	_Street Address_	_City_	_State_	_ZIP_

or ☐ I wish to keep the address confidential

Name	_Street Address_	_City_	_State_	_ZIP_

or ☐ I wish to keep the address confidential

☐ Other locations:

Name	_Street Address_	_City_	_State_	_ZIP_

or ☐ I wish to keep the address confidential

Name	_Street Address_	_City_	_State_	_ZIP_

or ☐ I wish to keep the address confidential

☐ c. School Restrictions
Fill in only if Respondent attends the same school as Petitioner.

_____ is an elementary, middle, or high school
School Name   attended by both Respondent and Petitioner.

Respondent be ordered _(check one)_:

☐ Not to attend Petitioner's school for as long as Petitioner is enrolled there;

☐ To accept a change of placement or program at Petitioner's school, as determined by the public school district or by a private or non-public school; or

☐ Not to be present in these parts of Petitioner's school:

_____
_____

☐ d. Requirements for Parents and Guardians
Respondent is a minor. To ensure that Respondent follows this _Order_, Respondent's Parent or Guardian:

_____
Name of Parent or Guardian

be ordered to: _____
_____

☐ **4. Counseling** _(available **only after** actual notice to Respondent and/or a hearing with the judge)_

Check if you want Respondent to get evaluation and treatment and all the boxes under it that apply.

NOTE: _A judge can only order counseling at a hearing where Respondent is present or has been given formal written notice._

☐ Respondent be ordered to participate in the following _(check all that apply)_:

☐ A Domestic Violence Partner Abuse program.

☐ An alcohol and substance abuse evaluation and to successfully complete all recommendations.

☐ A mental health evaluation and to successfully complete all recommendations.

☐ Other _(please specify)_: _____

INFORMATION ABOUT CHILDREN IN COMMON (SECTIONS 5-9)

> **Petitioner:** Fill out "Information about Children in Common" and Sections 5-9 only if you have children younger than 18 with Respondent.

☐ Both Petitioner (P) and Respondent (R) are the parents of these minor children:

Enter the names of all children under age 18 that you and Respondent have (or allegedly have) together.

NOTE: Legal parentage of a child may be established in the following ways: 1) There is a presumption of parentage because the parties are or were married or civilly united and the child was born during the marriage/union, within 300 days of its termination, or before the marriage/union and both parents' names have been added to their birth certificate. 2) Both parties have signed a Voluntary Acknowledgement of Paternity (VAP). 3) There is a court order or administrative order establishing parentage. 4) By giving birth to the child.

Child's Name *(first, middle, and last)*	Age	State of Residence	Legal Parentage Already Established for Petitioner (P) / Respondent (R)	Included as a Protected Person
_____	_____	_____	☐ - P ☐ - R ☐ Unsure	☐ Yes ☐ No
_____	_____	_____	☐ - P ☐ - R ☐ Unsure	☐ Yes ☐ No
_____	_____	_____	☐ - P ☐ - R ☐ Unsure	☐ Yes ☐ No
_____	_____	_____	☐ - P ☐ - R ☐ Unsure	☐ Yes ☐ No
_____	_____	_____	☐ - P ☐ - R ☐ Unsure	☐ Yes ☐ No
_____	_____	_____	☐ - P ☐ - R ☐ Unsure	☐ Yes ☐ No

I am asking the court to make decisions about the children because *(check all that apply)*:

☐ The children have lived in Illinois for the past six (6) months or if the children are younger than six (6) months old, they have lived in Illinois since they were born.

☐ I live in Illinois but someone else took the children out of Illinois within the past six (6) months. Before they were taken out of Illinois, the children lived here for at least six (6) months.

☐ The children are in Illinois because we fled here to avoid abuse of me or the children in another state.

☐ I'm not asking the court to make decisions about the children.

☐ The primary caretaker of the minor children is *(check one)*:

If the primary caretaker of the children is someone other than you or Respondent, check the box for "Other person" and enter that person's name and address.

☐ Petitioner ☐ Respondent

☐ Other person: _____
                    Name

_____
    Street, Apt. #   *City*   *State*   *ZIP*

☐ **5. Care and Possession of Children**

Check if you are protecting children you have with Respondent. Check the boxes that apply to your case and fill in the information.

If you do not want Respondent to know where the children go to school, check the last box and fill out the Confidential Name & Location of the School or Childcare Provider form, and file it with the Circuit Clerk as "confidential."

Petitioner requests the following *(check all that apply)*:

☐ Petitioner be granted physical care and possession of the minor children.

☐ Respondent be ordered to return the minor children to the physical care of Petitioner
or another person: _____.

☐ Respondent be ordered to not remove the minor children from the physical care of Petitioner or from a school or childcare provider.

☐ I have given the name and location of the school or childcare provider on the *Confidential Name & Location of the School or Childcare Provider* form.

☐ **6. Temporary Significant Decision-Making Responsibility** *(formerly custody)*

Check if you want significant decision-making responsibility (formerly custody).

*(This remedy is available **only after** actual notice to Respondent and/or a hearing with the judge)*

Petitioner requests temporary significant decision-making responsibility for the minor children.

☐ **7. Respondent's Parenting Time with the Minor Children** *(formerly visitation)*

*Check box **a, b, c,** or **d** to let the court know if, how, and when Respondent should have parenting time.*

Petitioner requests that the court order parenting time as follows *(check one—a, b, c, or d)*:

☐ a. GRANT parenting time for Respondent without restrictions *(if granting, fill out schedule below in part **7e**).*

☐ b. RESERVE parenting time until a later hearing *(this means the Court does not make any decisions on parenting time right now).* *(If you checked reserve, skip to Section **8**.)*

☐ c. DENY parenting time for Respondent —no visits at all. *(If you checked deny, **check your reason below** and then skip to **8**.)*

☐ d. RESTRICT parenting time for Respondent *(Visits with limits. **Check your reasons below,** then fill out the schedule below in **7e**.)*

*If you checked to **Deny** or **Restrict** in **7c** or **7d**, check all reasons that apply.*
Respondent is likely to *(check all that apply)*:

☐ Abuse or endanger the children during parenting time.

☐ Use parenting time to abuse or harass Petitioner, Petitioner's family, or household members.

☐ Improperly hide or detain the children.

☐ Act in a way that is not in the best interest of the children.

If you chose **Grant** or **Restrict**, request your parenting time schedule below:

*If you know what the schedule should be, either attach it and check **e1** or pick your parenting time schedule in **e2** below. Enter when, where, and how you want parenting time to happen and fill in the blanks with specific times, days, and other information. Include a.m. or p.m.*

☐ e. Respondent's parenting time should be *(check 1 or 2)*:

☐ 1. See attached parenting time schedule; or

☐ 2. The following parenting time schedule *(check all that apply)*:

☐ Every _____ from _____to _____
                 Weekdays   *Time*   *Time*

☐ Each weekend or ☐ Every other weekend as follows *(include am or pm)*:

from _____ at _____ to_____ at _____.
       Day of the Week   *Time*   *Day of the Week*   *Time*

☐ Parenting time is to begin on: _____
    Month, Day, Year

☐ Holidays (include date and times):

_____

_____

☐ The person responsible for transportation of the children for parenting time is:

_____
    Name

☐ Pickup for parenting time to take place at the following place:

Name of Place (if any)	*Street Address*	*City*	*State*

☐ Return from parenting time to take place at the following place:

Name of Place (if any)	*Street Address*	*City*	*State*

☐ Parenting time will take place at:

Name of Place (if any)	*Street Address*	*City*	*State*

☐ Parenting time will be supervised by: _____
    Name of Supervisor

who has filed or will file an *Affidavit of Parenting Time Supervisor* form with the court accepting responsibility and acknowledging accountability.

☐ Parenting time will be supervised at an official supervised visitation center *(if available)*.

☐ Respondent to return the children immediately at the end of parenting time to:
  ☐ Petitioner
  ☐ person chosen by Petitioner _____
       Name of Person Chosen by Petitioner

☐ 8. **No Concealment or Removal of Children**
Check if you are afraid Respondent will hide your children or take them out of state.

Respondent be ordered not to hide the children within the state or remove them from Illinois.

☐ 9. **Order to Appear** *(check all that apply)*

Respondent be ordered to appear in court ☐ alone ☐ with minor children to:
  ☐ Prevent abuse, neglect, removal or concealment of the children.
  ☐ Return the children to Petitioner.
  ☐ Permit a court-ordered interview or examination of the children or Respondent.

☐ 10. **Possession of Personal Property** *(check all that apply)*
Petitioner's Property:
Check if you want your things protected from Respondent. List things you want to keep with you.

☐ a. Petitioner be awarded possession of this property:

_____

_____

_____

_____

*Check if Respondent has some or all of the property you listed in **10a**. List the things you want back. Check all boxes below that apply to your case.*

☐ b. Respondent be ordered to give Petitioner

☐ all of the property listed in 10a above   or   ☐ the following property:

_____

_____

_____

_____

BECAUSE *(check one)*:

☐ Petitioner, but not Respondent, owns the property.

☐ Petitioner and Respondent both own the property. Sharing it would put Petitioner at risk for abuse or is not practical. Not having the property would be harder on Petitioner.

☐ The parties are married and a divorce case has been filed.

☐ c. Transfer of Personal Property

Property to be transferred at the following address:

_____	_____	_____	_____
Street, Apt. #	City	State	Zip

on _____ at _____ ☐ a.m. ☐ p.m.
      Month, Day, Year   Time

☐ Property to be transferred in the presence of *(check one)*:
Check who you want to be there when it happens and enter that person's name. It may be safer if the transfer is in the presence of a law enforcement officer.

☐ Law enforcement to be arranged by Petitioner

(Optional) ☐ _____;
         Name of Law Enforcement Agency

or

☐ Another adult: _____
         Name

☐ d. Respondent's Property

☐ Respondent be awarded possession of the following personal property: ☐ clothing ☐ medicine
☐ other personal property as follows:

_____

_____

_____

☐ Respondent have the right to enter the residence listed in Section **2** <u>only one time</u> to retrieve the property listed above, but only in the presence of: *(check one)*

☐ Law enforcement to be arranged by Respondent

(Optional) ☐ _____;
         Name of Law Enforcement Agency

or

☐ Another adult: _____
         Name

☐ **11. Restrictions on Property**

Check if you want your things protected from Respondent and list what you want protected. Then, check all the boxes below the lines that apply to your case.

List any property you want protected from the Respondent:

☐ Cars/Motor Vehicles *(Specify Make/Model/Year):* _____

☐ Address: _____

              Street, Apt. #   *City*   *State*

    ☐ Inside/Outside

    ☐ Items located inside

☐ Other important property:

_____

_____

BECAUSE *(check one):*

    ☐ Petitioner, but not Respondent, owns the property.

    ☐ Petitioner and Respondent both own the property. Not having the property would be harder on Petitioner.

    ☐ The parties are married and a divorce case has been filed.

☐ Restriction on Resources of an Elderly Petitioner

Check Restrictions on Resources to stop Respondent from using an elderly person's money or property for themselves.

    Respondent be ordered not to improperly use financial or other resources of an elderly Petitioner for the benefit of Respondent or any other person.

☐ **11.5. Possession of Animals**

Check to protect your pets from Respondent.

Petitioner be awarded possession of these animals *(include name, type and breed):*

_____

_____

Respondent should stay away from the animals and Respondent should be forbidden from taking, transferring, concealing, harming, or otherwise disposing of the animals.

☐ **12. Temporary Support** *(available **only after** actual notice to Respondent, and/or a hearing with the judge, check all that apply.)*

Check if you want Respondent to give you money to help you or children you have together. If you have it, bring proof of income to the next court date.

Respondent be ordered to pay support as follows:

    ☐ Respondent pay temporary child support.

    ☐ Respondent pay temporary maintenance *(formerly called spousal support or alimony).*

☐ **13. Payment for Losses because of Abuse** *(available **only after** actual notice to Respondent and/or a hearing with the judge, check all that apply.)*
Check all boxes that apply to your case. If you know, enter the amount of the cost in the blank. If you are not sure, you can estimate. Bring receipts, including proof of payment, and estimates of repairs to court if you have them.

Respondent be ordered to pay Petitioner for losses caused by abuse, neglect, or exploitation, including:

☐ Medical expense.. $_____

☐ Lost earnings.. $_____

☐ Repair or replace property damaged or taken.. $_____

☐ Moving and other travel expenses... $_____

☐ Reasonable expenses for housing other than a domestic violence shelter..................... $_____

☐ Expenses for search and recovery of children.. $_____

☐ Reasonable attorney's fees.. $_____

☐ Other:_____ $_____

☐ **14. No Entry of Presence Under Influence**

*If you checked any box in Section **2 (Possession of Residence)** or the first box in Section **3 (Stay Away)**, you cannot check box **14**.*

Respondent is allowed at the Petitioner's residence (below), but cannot be or stay there while under the influence of drugs or alcohol. This would be a threat to the safety or well-being of Petitioner or Petitioner's children.

_____

    Street, Apt. #   *City*   *State*

☐ **14.5. Firearms**

If you check any of the boxes below, make sure you explain in section G your concerns involving firearms and why you want firearms removed.

☐ **Surrender firearms**

Respondent should not be allowed to have firearms or firearm parts that could be used to assemble an operable firearm and should surrender any firearms or firearm parts, any Firearm Identification Owner (FOID) card, and any Concealed Carry License to law enforcement BECAUSE:

☐ Respondent poses a threat to Petitioner who is an intimate partner or Petitioner's child and we are asking for their guns to be taken away *(Civil order)*

☐ Respondent is or will be subject to a domestic violence order of protection entered under the Criminal Code *(Criminal orders)*

☐ **Search warrant**

A search warrant should be issued so that law enforcement can search Respondent's property and may seize firearms or firearm parts from the Respondent BECAUSE *(check all that apply)*:

☐ Respondent poses an immediate and present credible threat to the physical safety of the Petitioner.

☐ Respondent possesses a firearm or firearm parts that could be used to make a firearm.

☐ The firearm or firearm parts are in the residence, vehicle, or other property of the Respondent.

☐ Petitioner has made a credible report of domestic violence to local law enforcement within the last 90 days.

If seeking an Emergency Order of Protection (Ex Parte):

☐ Personal injury to the Petitioner is likely to occur if Respondent were to have prior notice of the Order of Protection.

☐ **15. Children's Records**

Check if you do not want Respondent to get your children's school records or other records. These records could provide Respondent with your protected address. Check all boxes that apply to your case.

Respondent should not be allowed to access, inspect, or obtain school records, healthcare records, or any other records of the children BECAUSE *(check all that apply)*:

☐ Petitioner is requesting that Respondent not be allowed to have contact with the minor children.

☐ The actual address of Petitioner is not included in this *Petition* due to the risk of further abuse.

☐ It is necessary to prevent abuse or wrongful removal or concealment of the children.

☐ **16. Shelter Reimbursement** *(available **only after** actual notice to Respondent and/or a hearing with the judge)*

In **16,** check if you want Respondent to pay the shelter. If you know, enter the amount of the cost in the blank. If you are not sure, you can estimate. Bring receipts to court if you have them.

Respondent be ordered to reimburse a shelter providing temporary

housing or counseling to Petitioner.. $_____

☐ **17. Miscellaneous Remedies**

Check if there are other things you want Respondent to do or to stop doing. List those things on the lines. Explain the reasons on the lines after "Because."

Respondent be ordered to:

_____

_____

_____

_____

_____

because:

_____

_____

_____

_____

_____

☐ **18. Telephone Services**

Check if you are on Respondent's cell phone plan and you want to separate your account. Enter the provider name and telephone numbers.

A wireless telephone provider should transfer from Respondent to Petitioner the right to continue to use their own telephone numbers and be responsible for the cost of them. Petitioner, or a minor child in Petitioner's custody, uses the telephone numbers.

Name of Provider: _____

Name of Account Holder: _____

Respondent Phone Number: _____

Petitioner's Phone Numbers: _____

_____

SIGN

Under 735 ILCS 5/1-109, your signature means that:

1) everything in this document is true and correct, or I have been informed or I believe it to be true and correct, and

2) I understand that making a false statement on this form is perjury and has penalties provided by law.

If you are filling out this form online, sign your name by typing it. If you are filling out this form by hand, sign and print your name

Your Signature /s/ _____ Print Your Name _____

Enter your complete address, telephone number, and email address if you have one. If you need to keep your addresses secret because of domestic violence, you may use another address. Those addresses must be ones at which you can receive mail about the case.

Contact Information for Notice Purposes:

Address _____
       Street, Apt. #   *City*   *State*   *Zip Code*

Phone Number _____

Email (if you have one) _____

Be sure to **check your email every day** so you do not miss important information, court dates, or documents from other parties.

Attorney Information (if any):

Attorney Name _____ Attorney Number (if any) _____

Attorney Signature_____

This pleading was prepared by the attorney above and executed in accordance with Supreme Court Rule 137.

DEFINITION OF TERMS

1. **Abuse** means physical abuse, harassment, intimidation of a dependent, interference with personal liberty or willful deprivation but does not include reasonable direction of a minor child by a parent or person in loco parentis.

2. **Adult with disabilities** means an elder adult with disabilities or a high-risk adult with disabilities. A person may be an adult with disabilities for purposes of this Act even though he or she has never been adjudicated an incompetent adult. However, no court proceeding may be initiated or continued on behalf of an adult with disabilities over that adult's objection, unless such proceeding is approved by his or her legal guardian, if any.

3. **Domestic violence** means abuse as defined in paragraph 1.

4. **Elder adult with disabilities** means an adult prevented by advanced age from taking appropriate action to protect himself or herself from abuse by a family or household member.

5. **Exploitation** means the illegal, including tortious, use of a high-risk adult with disabilities or of the assets or resources of a high-risk adult with disabilities. Exploitation includes, but is not limited to, the misappropriation of assets or resources of a high-risk adult with disabilities by undue influence, by breach of a fiduciary relationship, by fraud, deception, or extortion, or the use of such assets or resources in a manner contrary to law.

6. **Family or household members** include spouses, former spouses, parents, children, stepchildren and other persons related by blood or by present or prior marriage, persons who share or formerly shared a common dwelling, persons who have or allegedly have a child in common, persons who share or allegedly share a blood relationship through a child, persons who have or have had a dating or engagement relationship, persons with disabilities and their personal assistants, and caregivers as defined in Section 12-4.4a of the Criminal Code of 2012. For purposes of this paragraph, neither a casual acquaintanceship nor ordinary fraternization between 2 individuals in business or social contexts shall be deemed to constitute a dating relationship. In the case of a high-risk adult with disabilities, "family or household members" includes any person who has the responsibility for a high-risk adult as a result of a family relationship or who has assumed responsibility for all or a portion of the care of a high-risk adult with disabilities voluntarily, or by express or implied contract, or by court order.

7. **Harassment** means knowing conduct which is not necessary to accomplish a purpose that is reasonable under the circumstances; would cause a reasonable person emotional distress; and does cause emotional distress to the petitioner. Unless the presumption is rebutted by a preponderance of the evidence, the following types of conduct shall be presumed to cause emotional distress:
    a. creating a disturbance at petitioner's place of employment or school;
    b. repeatedly telephoning petitioner's place of employment, home or residence;
    c. repeatedly following petitioner about in a public place or places;
    d. repeatedly keeping petitioner under surveillance by remaining present outside his or her home, school, place of employment, vehicle or other place occupied by petitioner or by peering in petitioner's windows;
    e. improperly concealing a minor child from petitioner, repeatedly threatening to improperly remove a minor child of petitioner's from the jurisdiction or from the physical care of petitioner, repeatedly threatening to conceal a minor child from petitioner, or making a single such threat following an actual or attempted improper removal or concealment, unless respondent was fleeing an incident or pattern of domestic violence; or
    f. threatening physical force, confinement or restraint on one or more occasions.

8. **High-risk adult with disabilities** means a person aged 18 or over whose physical or mental disability impairs his or her ability to seek or obtain protection from abuse, neglect, or exploitation.

9. **Interference with personal liberty** means committing or threatening physical abuse, harassment, intimidation or willful deprivation so as to compel another to engage in conduct from which she or he has a right to abstain or to refrain from conduct in which she or he has a right to engage.

10. **Intimidation of a dependent** means subjecting a person who is dependent because of age, health or disability to participation in or the witnessing of: physical force against another or physical confinement or restraint of another which constitutes physical abuse as defined in this Act, regardless of whether the abused person is a family or household member.

11. **Neglect** means the failure to exercise that degree of care toward a high-risk adult with disabilities which a reasonable person would exercise under the circumstances and includes but is not limited to:
    a. the failure to take reasonable steps to protect a high-risk adult with disabilities from acts of abuse;
    b. the repeated, careless imposition of unreasonable confinement;
    c. the failure to provide food, shelter, clothing, and personal hygiene to a high-risk adult with disabilities who requires such assistance;
    d. the failure to provide medical and rehabilitative care for the physical and mental health needs of a high-risk adult with disabilities; or
    e. the failure to protect a high-risk adult with disabilities from health and safety hazards.

    Nothing in subsection 10 shall be construed to impose a requirement that assistance be provided to a high-risk adult with disabilities over his or her objection in the absence of a court order, nor to create any new affirmative duty to provide support to a high-risk adult with disabilities.

12. **Order of protection** means an emergency order, interim order or plenary order, granted pursuant to this Act, which includes any or all of the remedies authorized by Section 214 of this Act.

13. **Petitioner** may mean not only any named petitioner for the order of protection and any named victim of abuse on whose behalf the petition is brought, but also any other person protected by this Act.

14. **Physical abuse** includes sexual abuse and means any of the following:
    a. knowing or reckless use of physical force, confinement or restraint;
    b. knowing, repeated and unnecessary sleep deprivation; or
    c. knowing or reckless conduct which creates an immediate risk of physical harm.

14.5. **Stay away** means for the respondent to refrain from both physical presence and nonphysical contact with the petitioner whether direct, indirect (including, but not limited to, telephone calls, mail, email, faxes, and written notes), or through third parties who may or may not know about the order of protection.

15. **Willful deprivation** means willfully denying a person who because of age, health or disability requires medication, medical care, shelter, accessible shelter or services, food, therapeutic device, or other physical assistance, and thereby exposing that person to the risk of physical, mental or emotional harm, except with regard to medical care or treatment when the dependent person has expressed an intent to forgo such medical care or treatment. This paragraph does not create any new affirmative duty to provide support to dependent persons.

ADDITIONAL INCIDENTS OF ABUSE

(ORDER OF PROTECTION)

IN THE STATE OF ILLINOIS, CIRCUIT COURT

COUNTY: _____
County Where You Are Filing the Case

Enter the case information as it appears on your other court documents.

PETITIONER: _____
Who started the case.   First, Middle, and Last Name

Filing on behalf of a ☐ minor or ☐ high-risk adult: _____

RESPONDENT: _____
Who you are seeking protection from.   First, Middle, and Last Name

_____
Case Number

⚠ Use this **only** if you run out of space in section G on your *Petition*. If you need more space, attach more than one *Additional Incidents of Abuse* forms or your own extra pages. File it with your *Petition*.

Additional Incidents of Abuse continued from the *Petition for Order of Protection*:

G. An *Order of Protection* is needed because Respondent did these things:
    *It is important to be as detailed as you can, with times and dates if you know them or as close as possible. **Include facts that support or explain whatever protections you are asking for.** Start with the most recent incident or event that caused you to file this Petition.*

Date: _____ Time: _____ Description of what happened:

_____
_____
_____
_____
_____
_____

Date: _____ Time: _____ Description of what happened:

_____
_____
_____
_____
_____
_____

Date: _____ Time: _____ Description of what happened:

_____
_____
_____
_____
_____
_____

This form is approved by the Illinois Supreme Court and is required to be accepted in all Illinois Circuit Courts. Forms are free at ilcourts.info/forms.
ATJ 408.3   Page 1 of 2   (05/25)

46

Date: _____Time: _____ Description of what happened:

_____
_____
_____
_____
_____
_____

Date: _____Time: _____ Description of what happened:

_____
_____
_____
_____
_____
_____

Date: _____Time: _____ Description of what happened:

_____
_____
_____
_____
_____
_____

Date: _____Time: _____ Description of what happened:

_____
_____
_____
_____
_____
_____

Date: _____Time: _____ Description of what happened:

_____
_____
_____
_____
_____
_____

File this form with your *Petition for Order of Protection.*

ADDITIONAL CASE INFORMATION

(ORDER OF PROTECTION)

IN THE STATE OF ILLINOIS, CIRCUIT COURT

COUNTY: _____

County Where You Are Filing the Case

Enter the case information as it appears on your other court documents.

PETITIONER: _____

Who started the case.   First, Middle, and Last Name

Filing on behalf of a ☐ minor or ☐ high-risk adult: _____

Case Number

RESPONDENT: _____

Who you are seeking protection from.   First, Middle, and Last Name

Additional Case Information continued from the *Order of Protection*:

E. Is there now, or has there ever been, another *Order of Protection* entered between Petitioner and Respondent?

☐ Yes   ☐ No   ☐ Do not know

If yes, list information about the cases:

Names of People Involved	County & State	Year	Case No.	Pending?
				☐ Yes ☐ No
				☐ Yes ☐ No
				☐ Yes ☐ No
				☐ Yes ☐ No
				☐ Yes ☐ No
				☐ Yes ☐ No

F. Is there now, or has there ever been, another court case between Petitioner and Respondent?

List all other types of court cases that you have been involved in with Respondent, such as divorce, custody, child support, parentage, parenting time, guardianship, adoption, criminal, or abuse and neglect cases.

☐ Yes   ☐ No   ☐ Do not know

If yes, list information about the cases:

Names of People Involved	County & State	Year	Case No.	Pending?
				☐ Yes ☐ No
				☐ Yes ☐ No
				☐ Yes ☐ No
				☐ Yes ☐ No
				☐ Yes ☐ No
				☐ Yes ☐ No

File this form with your *Petition for Order of Protection*.

This form is approved by the Illinois Supreme Court and is required to be accepted in all Illinois Circuit Courts. Forms are free at ilcourts.info/forms.

ATJ 409.3   Page 1 of 1   (05/25)

CONFIDENTIAL NAME & LOCATION OF THE SCHOOL OR DAYCARE

(ORDER OF PROTECTION)
IN THE STATE OF ILLINOIS, CIRCUIT COURT

COUNTY: _____
County Where You Are Filing the Case

Enter the case information as it appears on your other court documents.

PETITIONER: _____
Who started the case.   First, Middle, and Last Name

Filing on behalf of a ☐ minor or ☐ high-risk adult: _____

RESPONDENT: _____
Who you are seeking protection from.   First, Middle, and Last Name

_____
Case Number

Petitioner:
- ○ Use this form only if you did not list the addresses of schools or daycares in your Petition because you do not want Respondent to know these addresses.
- ○ Tell the Circuit Clerk this document is confidential or e-file it as "confidential."

Within 24 hours of this *Order* being entered, the Circuit Clerk shall send written notice of the *Order* to the following:
Enter the location name, address and the children's names.

1. Location Name: _____

    Children at this Location: _____

    Location is a ☐ School ☐ Daycare

    Address: _____
    Street Address   City   State   ZIP

2. Location Name: _____

    Children at this Location: _____

    Location is a ☐ School ☐ Daycare

    Address: _____
    Street Address   City   State   ZIP

3. Location Name: _____

    Children at this Location: _____

    Location is a ☐ School ☐ Daycare

    Address: _____
    Street Address   City   State   ZIP

4. Location Name: _____

    Children at this Location: _____

    Location is a ☐ School ☐ Daycare

    Address: _____
    Street Address   City   State   ZIP

This form is approved by the Illinois Supreme Court and must be accepted in all Illinois Courts. Forms are free at ilcourts.info/forms.
ATJ 411.3   Page 1 of 1   (05/25)

49

AFFIDAVIT OF PARENTING TIME SUPERVISOR

(ORDER OF PROTECTION)

IN THE STATE OF ILLINOIS, CIRCUIT COURT

COUNTY: _____
County Where You Are Filing the Case

Enter the case information as it appears on your other court documents.

PETITIONER: _____
Who started the case.   *First, Middle, and Last Name*

Filing on behalf of a ☐ minor or ☐ high-risk adult: _____

RESPONDENT: _____
Who you are seeking protection from.   *First, Middle, and Last Name*

_____
Case Number

Parenting time supervisor completes this form.

I, _____ , state as follows:
Supervisor's First Middle Last

1. I reside at: _____
   Street Address, Apt #   *City*   *State*   *ZIP*

2. My telephone number is: _____ .

3. My relationship to the parties is: _____ .

4. I accept the responsibility to be present at all times and to supervise Respondent's parenting time according to the court's Order with these children:

   _____
   Children's Names

5. By signing this affidavit I submit to the jurisdiction of the court and certify that I will require Respondent to follow these rules during parenting time:
   - No discussion with the children about any court cases or any *Petition for Order of Protection*;
   - No discussion with the children about the custodial parent's activities;
   - No use of alcohol or drugs;
   - No abusive language;
   - No hitting, striking, or other violent physical contact;
   - No physical discipline; and
   - No threatening behavior.

6. I will cancel the parenting time session if Respondent arrives under the influence of alcohol or drugs.

7. I will end a parenting time session if Respondent violates any of the rules listed above or it is otherwise necessary to protect the children's safety or best interests.

8. I understand that I am responsible to the court for carrying out the duties listed in this Affidavit.

SIGN

Under 735 ILCS 5/1-109, your signature means that:

1) everything in this document is true and correct, or I have been informed or I believe it to be true and correct, and

2) I understand that making a false statement on this form is perjury and has penalties provided by law.

If you are filling out this form online, sign your name by typing it. If you are filling out this form by hand, sign and print your name.

Your Signature /s/ _____   Print Your Name _____

This form is approved by the Illinois Supreme Court and must be accepted in all Illinois Courts. Forms are free at ilcourts.info/forms.

ATJ 410.3   Page 1 of 1   (05/25)

50

EMERGENCY ORDER
OF PROTECTION

IN THE STATE OF ILLINOIS, CIRCUIT COURT

COUNTY: _____
County Where You Are Filing the Case

Enter the case information as it appears on your other court documents.

PETITIONER: _____
Who started the case.   First, Middle, and Last Name

Filing on behalf of a ☐ minor or ☐ high-risk adult: _____

RESPONDENT: _____
Who you are seeking protection from.   First, Middle, and Last Name

Case Number

People to be Protected by this *Order*:

Check the boxes for **all** people you want to include in the *Order*

☐ Petitioner: _____

☐ Petitioner's minor children with Respondent:

_____

_____

☐ Petitioner's other minor children:

_____

_____

☐ Dependent adult: _____

☐ High-risk adult: _____

☐ Other household members:

_____

_____

☐ Civil / Emergency Proceeding

_____
Related Civil Case Number (if known)

☐ Criminal / Ex parte Proceeding

_____
Related Criminal or Delinquency Case Number (if known)

ORDER INFORMATION:

☐ This *Order* was issued on: _____ at _____ ☐ a.m. ☐ p.m.
Month, Day, Year   *Time*

☐ Civil Case: this *Order* will end on: _____ at _____ ☐ a.m. ☐ p.m.
Month, Day, Year   *Time*

☐ Criminal Case: this *Order* will be in effect until the hearing on a final protective *Order*.

NEXT COURT DATE:

_____ at _____ ☐ a.m. ☐ p.m. in _____.
Month, Day, Year   *Time*   *Courtroom Number*

Look at page 2 for more information on how to attend court.

This form is approved by the Illinois Supreme Court and must be accepted in all Illinois Courts. Forms are free at ilcourts.info/forms.
ATJ 404.4   Page 1 of 14   (05/25)

Court dates may be scheduled in-person, remotely, or a combination of in-person and remotely. Find out how your court date will be scheduled and provide that information here. Add the Clerk's phone number and website.

Attend court any of the ways checked:

☐ **In person** at: _____
                 Courtroom Address   *Courtroom Number*

☐ **Remotely** *(video or telephone option)*

      By video conference at: _____
                                Video Conference Website

          Log-in information: _____
                           Video Conference Log-in Information, Meeting ID, Password, etc.

      By telephone at: _____
                    Call-in Number for Telephone Remote Appearance

To find out more about remote court options:

Phone: _____ or Website: _____
      Circuit Clerk's Phone Number   *Website URL*

> **Respondent:** A *Plenary* (long-term) *Order of Protection* may be entered if you (Respondent) do not come to this hearing.

> **Petitioner:** If you are completing this form for a minor child, a dependent adult, or a high-risk adult, provide that person's information on this form instead of your own information.

A. Petitioner's ☐ **residential address or** ☐ **alternative address for notice** (residential address is undisclosed)

_____
Street, Apt #   *City*   *State*   *ZIP*

_____
Email

B. Respondent's Information *(if known)*:

Date of Birth: _____ Sex: _____ Race: _____

Respondent's Home address:

_____
   Street, Apt #   *City*   *State*   *ZIP*

Respondent's Email: _____

Respondent's work information, including when usually works:

_____
   Respondent's Employer Name   *Respondent's Work Hours*

_____
   Respondent Employer Street Address   *City*   *State*   *ZIP*

Other Respondent identifiers:

_____ _____ _____ _____
Height   *Weight*   *Hair Color*   *Eye Color*

Any distinguishing features of the Respondent (for example: scars, marks, or tattoos?

_____

THE COURT ORDERS THAT YOU OBEY ALL SECTIONS SELECTED BELOW:

☐ 1. **No Abuse** **(R01) (Police Enforced)**

Respondent shall not threaten or commit the following acts of abuse towards Petitioner and protected people. *(check all that apply)*:

☐ Harassment   ☐ Intimidation of a Dependent

☐ Physical Abuse   ☐ Exploitation of a High-Risk Adult with Disabilities

☐ Stalking   ☐ Neglect of a High-Risk Adult with Disabilities

☐ Willful Deprivation   ☐ Interference with Personal Liberty

☐ 2. **Possession of Residence** **(R02) (Police Enforced)**

Petitioner is granted exclusive possession of the residence and Respondent is ordered not to stay or be at the residence. These remedies do not affect who owns the property, only who gets to use or occupy it.

Petitioner's residence is located at *(check one):*

☐ Petitioner's address is confidential and omitted from these forms.

or

☐ _____
      Street, Apt #   City   State   ZIP

The court finds:

☐ Petitioner has a right to occupy the residence and Respondent has no right; or

☐ Petitioner and Respondent both have the right to occupy the residence, but it would be harder on the Petitioner to leave after considering the factors set forth in 750 ILCS 60/214(b)(2)(B) or 725 ILCS 5/112A-14(b)(2)(B).

Provision of alternate housing. Not available in an Emergency Order.

☐ 3. **Stay Away from Petitioner, Protected People, and Certain Places** **(R03) (Police Enforced)**

☐ Respondent shall stay away from Petitioner and protected people at all times, and shall not have any contact, including through third parties.

> **Respondent:** If ordered to stay away from Petitioner and protected people, you (Respondent) must not have ANY physical, non-physical, direct, or indirect contact with Petitioner and protected people. This includes oral communication, written communication, sign language, telephone and cell phone calls, faxes, texts, tweets, emails, posts, or communication by any other social media, and all other communication with Petitioner and protected people. This also includes contact or communication through others who may not know about the *Order of Protection.*

☐ Respondent shall not be at or stay at any of these places while Petitioner is there:

☐ Places of employment of Petitioner, located at:

_____   _____
Name   Street Address   City   State   ZIP

or ☐ Address is confidential and is omitted from these forms.

_____   _____
Name   Street Address   City   State   ZIP

or ☐ Address is confidential and is omitted from these forms.

☐ Schools, kindergartens, or daycare centers of Petitioner, located at:

_____   _____
Name   *Street Address*   *City*   *State*   *ZIP*

or ☐ Address is confidential and is omitted from these forms.

_____   _____
Name   *Street Address*   *City*   *State*   *ZIP*

or ☐ Address is confidential and is omitted from these forms.

☐ Other locations:

_____   _____
Name   *Street Address*   *City*   *State*   *ZIP*

or ☐ Address is confidential and is omitted from these forms.

_____   _____
Name   *Street Address*   *City*   *State*   *ZIP*

or ☐ Address is confidential and is omitted from these forms.

☐ School Restrictions
Fill in only if Respondent attends the same school as Petitioner.

_____ is an elementary, middle, or high school
School Name   attended by both Respondent and Petitioner.

After considering the factors in 750 ILCS 60/214(b)(3)(B):

☐ Respondent shall not attend this school for as long as Petitioner is enrolled there;

☐ Respondent shall accept a change of placement or program at this school as determined by the public school district or by this private or non-public school; OR

☐ Respondent shall follow these restrictions on movement within the school:

_____

_____

_____

☐ Requirements for Parents and Guardians
Respondent is a minor. To ensure that Respondent follows this *Order*, Respondent's Parent or Guardian:

_____
Name of Parent or Guardian

must do the following: _____

_____

4. **Counseling** *Not available in an Emergency Order.*

INFORMATION ABOUT CHILDREN IN COMMON (SECTIONS 5-9)

NOTE: Legal parentage of a child may be established in the following ways: 1) There is a presumption of parentage because the parties are or were married or civilly united and the child was born during the marriage/union, within 300 days of its termination, or before the marriage/union and both parents' names have been added to their birth certificate. 2) Both parties have signed a Voluntary Acknowledgement of Paternity (VAP). 3) There is a court order or administrative order establishing parentage. 4) By giving birth to the child.

Child's Name *(first, middle, last)*	Age	State of Residence	Legal Parentage Already Established for Petitioner (P) / Respondent (R)	Included as a Protected Person
_____	___	_____	☐ - P ☐ - R ☐ Unsure	☐ Yes ☐ No
_____	___	_____	☐ - P ☐ - R ☐ Unsure	☐ Yes ☐ No
_____	___	_____	☐ - P ☐ - R ☐ Unsure	☐ Yes ☐ No
_____	___	_____	☐ - P ☐ - R ☐ Unsure	☐ Yes ☐ No
_____	___	_____	☐ - P ☐ - R ☐ Unsure	☐ Yes ☐ No
_____	___	_____	☐ - P ☐ - R ☐ Unsure	☐ Yes ☐ No

☐ The court finds the primary caretaker of the minor children is *(check one)*:
If the primary caretaker of the children is someone other than you or Respondent, check the box for "Other person" and enter that person's name and address.

  ☐ Petitioner ☐ Respondent

  ☐ Other person:

_____ _____ _____ _____ _____
Name of Person   *Street, Apt #*   *City*   *State*   *ZIP*

☐ The court finds it does not have jurisdiction over the children.

☐ The court finds it has jurisdiction over the children because:

  ☐ The children have lived in Illinois for the past six (6) months or if the children are younger than six (6) months old, they have lived in Illinois since they were born.

  ☐ Petitioner lives in Illinois but someone else took the children out of Illinois within the past six (6) months. Before they were taken out of Illinois, the children lived here for at least six (6) months.

  ☐ The children are in Illinois because Petitioner fled here to avoid abuse in another state.

  ☐ Other: _____

☐ **5. Care and Possession of Children**   **(R05) Police/Court Enforced**

  ☐ Petitioner is granted physical care and possession of the minor children.

  ☐ Respondent shall, personally or through a law enforcement agency as authorized by the court, return the minor children to the physical care of:

  ☐ Petitioner

  ☐ Other person:

_____ _____ _____ _____ _____
Name of Person   *Street, Apt #*   *City*   *State*   *ZIP*

  ☐ Respondent shall not remove the minor children from the physical care of Petitioner or from a school or childcare provider. The names of the schools or providers are:

_____
Name of School or Childcare Provider

☐ Within 24 hours of this Order being entered, the Circuit Clerk shall send written notice of the Order to the following school, daycare, or health care providers:

Name of Place	Street Address	City	State
Name of Place	Street Address	City	State
Name of Place	Street Address	City	State

☐ For the safety of Petitioner, the name and location of the school or daycare are listed on the Confidential Name & Location of the School or Childcare Provider form.

6. **Temporary Significant Decision-Making Responsibility.** Not available in an Emergency Order.

☐ 7. **Respondent's Parenting Time** *(formerly visitation)* **with the Minor Children**   **(R07) (Court Enforced)**

Parenting time is:

☐ GRANTED for the Respondent *(without any restrictions listed below)*.

☐ RESERVED until a later hearing *(The Court does not make ANY decision on parenting time right now)*.

   ☐ Associated with family case: _____.

☐ DENIED *(No visits at all)*.

☐ RESTRICTED *(Visits with limits as listed below)*.

   If parenting time is DENIED or RESTRICTED, check the reasons below:

   Respondent is likely to *(check all that apply)*:

   ☐ Abuse or endanger the children during parenting time.

   ☐ Use parenting time to abuse or harass Petitioner, Petitioner's family, or household members.

   ☐ Improperly hide or detain the children.

   ☐ Act in a way that is not in the best interest of the children.

☐ Parenting time is GRANTED or RESTRICTED as follows *(check the box that applies)*:

   ☐ See attached parenting time schedule; OR

   ☐ The parenting time schedule is *(check all that apply, include a.m. or p.m.)*:

      ☐ Every _____ from _____ to _____
               Weekdays   *Time*   *Time*

      ☐ Each weekend OR ☐ Every other weekend as follows *(include a.m. or p.m.)*:

         ☐ from: _____ at _____ to _____ at _____
             Day of the Week   *Time*   *Day of the Week*   *Time*

      ☐ Parenting time is to begin on: _____
                            Month, Day, Year

      ☐ Holidays (include date and times):

      _____

      _____

   ☐ The person responsible for transportation of the children for parenting time is:

   _____
      Name

   ☐ Pickup for parenting time to take place at the following place:

Name of Place (if any)	Street Address	City	State

☐ Return from parenting time to take place at the following place:

_____ _____ _____ _____
Name of Place (if any)   *Street Address*   *City*   *State*

☐ Parenting time will take place at:

_____ _____ _____ _____
Name of Place (if any)   *Street Address*   *City*   *State*

☐ Parenting time will be supervised by: _____
                                          Name of Supervisor

who has filed or will file an *Affidavit of Parenting Time Supervisor* form with the court accepting responsibility and acknowledging accountability.

☐ Parenting time will be supervised at an official supervised visitation center *(if available)*:

_____
Name of Visitation Center

☐ Respondent to return the children immediately at the end of parenting time to:

☐ Petitioner

☐ Person chosen by Petitioner: _____
                                Name of Person Chosen by Petitioner

> **Respondent:** Petitioner may, by law, deny you (Respondent) access to the minor children if, when you arrive for parenting time, you are under the influence of drugs or alcohol and constitute a threat to the safety and well-being of Petitioner or the minor children of Petitioner or you are behaving in a violent or abusive manner (750 ILCS 60/214(b)(7)).

☐ **8. No Concealment or Removal of Children** **(R08) (Police Enforced)**

Respondent shall not hide the minor children within the State or remove the children from Illinois.

☐ **9. Order to Appear** **(R09) (Court Enforced)**

Respondent shall appear ☐ alone ☐ with minor children at the Courthouse:

_____ _____ _____ _____
Name of Courthouse   *Street Address*   *City*   *State*

in Courtroom _____ on _____ at _____ ☐ a.m. ☐ p.m.
          Courtroom   *Date*   *Time*

to *(check all that apply)*:

☐ Prevent abuse, neglect, removal or concealment of the children.

☐ Return the children to the custody or care of Petitioner.

☐ Permit a court-ordered interview or examination of the children or Respondent.

☐ **10. Possession of Personal Property** *(does not affect ownership of property)* **(R10) (Court Enforced)**

Petitioner's Property:

☐ Petitioner is awarded possession of this property:

_____
_____
_____

☐ Respondent be ordered to give Petitioner
☐ all of the property listed above ☐ the following:

_____
_____
_____

☐ property given to _____.
                     Name of Person

The Court finds as follows:

☐ Petitioner, but not Respondent, owns the property; or

☐ Petitioner and Respondent both own the property. Sharing it would put Petitioner at risk for abuse, or is not practical. Not having the property would be harder on Petitioner; or

☐ Petitioner claims the property as marital property, and a divorce case has been filed.

☐ Property shall be transferred at the following address:

_____

| Street, Apt # | City | State | ZIP |

on _____ at _____ ☐ a.m. ☐ p.m.

| Month, Day, Year | | Time | |

☐ Property shall be transferred only in the presence of:

   ☐ Law enforcement to be arranged by Petitioner

      (Optional) ☐ _____ ;

            Name of Law Enforcement Agency

  or

   ☐ Another adult: _____

            Name

Respondent's Property

☐ Respondent is awarded possession of the following personal property: ☐ clothing ☐ medicine

☐ other personal property as follows:

_____

_____

_____

☐ Respondent shall have the right to enter the residence listed in Section **2** only one time to retrieve the property listed above, but only in the presence of: (check one)

   ☐ Law enforcement to be arranged by Respondent

      (Optional) ☐ _____ ;

            Name of Law Enforcement Agency

  or

   ☐ Another adult: _____

            Name

☐ **11. Restrictions on Property**   **(R11) (Court Enforced)**

The Respondent shall not take, transfer, encumber, conceal, hide, damage, or otherwise dispose of any real or personal property, except as explicitly authorized by the Court. The following property is protected:

   ☐ Cars/Motor Vehicles (*Specify Make/Model/Year*): _____

   ☐ Address: _____

          Street, Apt #   *City*   *State*   *ZIP*

      ☐ Inside/Outside

      ☐ Items located inside

   ☐ Other important property:

_____

_____

BECAUSE *(check one)*:

   ☐ Petitioner, but not Respondent, owns the property.

   ☐ Petitioner and Respondent both own the property. Not having the property would be harder on Petitioner.

   ☐ The parties are married and a divorce case has been filed.

☐ Restrictions on Resources of an Elderly Petitioner
Respondent is prohibited from improperly using financial or other resources of an elderly Petitioner for the benefit of Respondent or any other person.

☐ **11.5 Possession of Animals** **(R11.5) (Court Enforced)**
Petitioner shall have care, custody, and control over the following animals (*include name, type and breed*):

_____

_____

Respondent shall stay away from the animals and Respondent is forbidden from taking, transferring, concealing, harming, or otherwise disposing of the animals.

12. Temporary Support. *Not available in an Emergency Order.*

13. Payment for Losses because of Abuse. *Not available in an Emergency Order.*

☐ **14. No Entry or Presence Under Influence** **(R14) (Police Enforced)**
Respondent is allowed at the Petitioner's residence but cannot be or stay there while under the influence of drugs or alcohol, and constitutes a threat to the safety of Petitioner or Petitioner's children:

Street, Apt #	City	State	ZIP

Respondent: Under Illinois law, while any Order of Protection is in effect, your (Respondent's) FOID card will be automatically suspended, revoked or denied and you are automatically prohibited from acquiring or possessing a firearm (per 430 ILCS 65/8.2). Your conceal and carry license is also suspended while the Order is in effect and must be turned over to the Court or law enforcement (per 430 ILCS 66/70B).

When an Order ends, you can request the return of your firearms and FOID card as long as your FOID card is not expired and there is no other order restricting your possession of firearms.

☐ **14.5. Firearms** **(R14.5) (Police Enforced)**
Respondent is prohibited from possessing firearms for the duration of this Order. Respondent must immediately surrender to law enforcement (and not transfer to a third party) any firearms, firearm parts that could be assembled to make an operable firearm, Firearm Owner Identification (FOID) Card, and/or Concealed Carry License. If these items are not in Respondent's possession at time of service, they must be surrendered to law enforcement (and not transferred to a third party) within 24 hours.

The Court finds as follows:

Civil Orders:
☐ Petitioner has satisfied the requirements of Section 217 of the Illinois Domestic Violence Act and good causes exists to grant this remedy.
☐ Personal injury to the Petitioner is likely to occur if Respondent had prior notice of the Order of Protection.
☐ This Order restrains Respondent from using physical force, harassment, stalking, or threatening an intimate partner or child of an intimate partner.
☐ Respondent poses a credible threat to the physical safety of Petitioner.
☐ Probable cause exists to believe that:
  ☐ Respondent possesses firearms or firearm parts that could be assembled to make an operable firearm.
  ☐ The firearms or firearm parts that could be assembled to make an operable firearm are located at the residence, vehicle, or other property of the Respondent.
  ☐ The credible threat to the physical safety of Petitioner is immediate and present.
☐ Petitioner has made a credible report of domestic violence to local law enforcement within the last 90 days.

Criminal Orders:

☐ Petitioner has satisfied the requirements of Section 112A-17.5 of the Code of Criminal Procedure and good cause exists to grant this remedy.

☐ Personal injury to the Petitioner is likely to occur if Respondent were to have prior notice.

☐ Respondent is subject to this domestic violence order of protection and may not lawfully possess firearms, firearm parts, or a FOID card under Section 8.2 of the Firearm Owners Identification Act.

☐ Probable cause exists to believe that:

    ☐ Respondent possesses firearms or firearm parts that could be assembled to make an operable firearm.

    ☐ The firearms or firearm parts that could be assembled to make an operable firearm are located at the residence, vehicle, or other property of the Respondent.

    ☐ Respondent poses an immediate and present credible threat to Petitioner.

☐ **15. Children's Records**   **(R15) (Court Enforced)**

Respondent is not allowed to access, inspect, or obtain school records or any other records of the minor children in the care of Petitioner because *(check all that apply)*:

☐ This *Order of Protection* prohibits Respondent from having contact with the minor children.

☐ The actual address of Petitioner is not included due to the risk of further abuse.

☐ It is necessary to prevent abuse or wrongful removal or concealment of the minor children.

16. Shelter Reimbursement. *Not available in an Emergency Order.*

☐ **17. Miscellaneous Remedies**   **(R17) (Court Enforced)**

The court further orders as follows:

_____

_____

_____

_____

_____

_____

☐ **18. Telephone Services**   **(R18) (Court Enforced)**

After considering the evidence, the wireless telephone service provider shall terminate Respondent's use of Petitioner's phone number, transfer to Petitioner the right to use these phone numbers, and transfer to Petitioner all financial responsibility associated with future use of these phone numbers.

Wireless telephone provider account details:

Name of Provider: _____

Name of Account Holder: _____

Respondent's Phone Number: _____

Petitioner's Phone Numbers: _____

_____

STOP Petitioner: STOP! Only the Judge or Circuit Clerk should write anything below this point.

After reviewing the *Petition* and hearing the evidence and testimony of Petitioner, the Court makes findings which:

☐ Are written on page 13 and 14 of this *Order*; or

☐ Were made orally and videotaped or recorded by a court reporter and are incorporated into this *Order*.

ENTERED:

_____   _____
             Judge   *Date*

I hereby certify that this is a true and correct copy of the original order on file with the Court.

Clerk of the Circuit Court of _____ County, Illinois _____

Date

_____

Seal (and signature, as locally required)

Copies given to: ☐ Petitioner ☐ Respondent in Open Court ☐ State's Attorney

Clerk to send copies to Sheriff to: ☐ serve Respondent
☐ enter into LEADS

Order drafted by

Attorney: _____

| *Name* | *Address* | *Telephone* | *Attorney Number (if any)* |

If you want to contest this Order of Protection you must:

Emergency Order of Protection (Civil Case)
- File a motion with the court stating:
  1) you did not receive prior notice, and
  2) you have a valid defense to the *Order*, or
  3) the *Order*, or any of its remedies, was not authorized under the law.

Ex Parte Protective Order (Criminal Case)
- File a written notice with the court stating you have a meritorious *(valid)* defense.
- Written notice must include an Affidavit providing the evidence of your meritorious *(valid)* defense. You must bring this evidence to the hearing.

Notices About Enforcement:

A violation of this order may result in fine or imprisonment.

Any knowing violation of an *Order of Protection* forbidding physical abuse, neglect, exploitation, harassment, intimidation, interference with personal liberty, willful deprivation, or entering or remaining present at specified places when any Protected Persons are present, or granting exclusive possession of the residence or household or granting a stay away order is a Class A misdemeanor. Grants of exclusive possession of the residence or household shall constitute notice forbidding trespass to land. Any knowing violation of an order awarding parental responsibility (formerly custody) or physical care of a child or care of a child or prohibiting removal or concealment of a child may be a Class 4 felony. Any willful violation of any order is contempt of court.

This *Order of Protection* is enforceable, even without registration, in all 50 states, the District of Columbia, tribal lands, and the U.S. Territories pursuant to the Violence Against Women Act (18 U.S.C. § 2265), provided notice of this *Order of Protection* has been provided to the Respondent. Violating this *Order of Protection* may subject the Respondent to state and/or federal charges and punishment. 18 U.S.C. §§ 2261-2262.

DEFINITION OF TERMS USED IN THIS *ORDER*

1. **Abuse** means physical abuse, harassment, intimidation of a dependent, interference with personal liberty or willful deprivation but does not include reasonable direction of a minor child by a parent or person in loco parentis.

2. **Adult with disabilities** means an elder adult with disabilities or a high-risk adult with disabilities. A person may be an adult with disabilities for purposes of this Act even though he or she has never been adjudicated an incompetent adult. However, no court proceeding may be initiated or continued on behalf of an adult with disabilities over that adult's objection, unless such proceeding is approved by his or her legal guardian, if any.

3. **Elder adult with disabilities** means an adult prevented by advanced age from taking appropriate action to protect himself or herself from abuse by a family or household member.

4. **Exploitation** means the illegal, including tortious, use of a high-risk adult with disabilities or of the assets or resources of a high-risk adult with disabilities. Exploitation includes, but is not limited to, the misappropriation of assets or resources of a high-risk adult with disabilities by undue influence, by breach of a fiduciary relationship, by fraud, deception, or extortion, or the use of such assets or resources in a manner contrary to law.

5. **Family or household members** include spouses, former spouses, parents, children, stepchildren and other persons related by blood or by present or prior marriage, persons who share or formerly shared a common dwelling, persons who have or allegedly have a child in common, persons who share or allegedly share a blood relationship through a child, persons who have or have had a dating or engagement relationship, persons with disabilities and their personal assistants, and caregivers as defined in Section 12-4.4a of the Criminal Code of 2012. For purposes of this paragraph, neither a casual acquaintanceship nor ordinary fraternization between 2 individuals in business or social contexts shall be deemed to constitute a dating relationship. In the case of a high-risk adult with disabilities, "family or household members" includes any person who has the responsibility for a high-risk adult as a result of a family relationship or who has assumed responsibility for all or a portion of the care of a high-risk adult with disabilities voluntarily, or by express or implied contract, or by court order.

6. **Harassment** means knowing conduct which is not necessary to accomplish a purpose that is reasonable under the circumstances; would cause a reasonable person emotional distress; and does cause emotional distress to the petitioner. Unless the presumption is rebutted by a preponderance of the evidence, the following types of conduct shall be presumed to cause emotional distress:
   a. creating a disturbance at petitioner's place of employment or school;
   b. repeatedly telephoning petitioner's place of employment, home or residence;
   c. repeatedly following petitioner about in a public place or places;
   d. repeatedly keeping petitioner under surveillance by remaining present outside his or her home, school, place of employment, vehicle or other place occupied by petitioner or by peering in petitioner's windows;
   e. improperly concealing a minor child from petitioner, repeatedly threatening to improperly remove a minor child of petitioner's from the jurisdiction or from the physical care of petitioner, repeatedly threatening to conceal a minor child from petitioner, or making a single such threat following an actual or attempted improper removal or concealment, unless respondent was fleeing an incident or pattern of domestic violence; or
   f. threatening physical force, confinement or restraint on one or more occasions.

7. **High-risk adult with disabilities** means a person aged 18 or over whose physical or mental disability impairs his or her ability to seek or obtain protection from abuse, neglect, or exploitation.

8. **Interference with personal liberty** means committing or threatening physical abuse, harassment, intimidation or willful deprivation so as to compel another to engage in conduct from which she or he has a right to abstain or to refrain from conduct in which she or he has a right to engage.

9. **Intimidation of a dependent** means subjecting a person who is dependent because of age, health or disability to participation in or the witnessing of: physical force against another or physical confinement or restraint of another which constitutes physical abuse as defined in this Act, regardless of whether the abused person is a family or household member.

10. **Neglect** means the failure to exercise that degree of care toward a high-risk adult with disabilities which a reasonable person would exercise under the circumstances and includes but is not limited to:
    a. the failure to take reasonable steps to protect a high-risk adult with disabilities from acts of abuse;
    b. the repeated, careless imposition of unreasonable confinement;
    c. the failure to provide food, shelter, clothing, and personal hygiene to a high-risk adult with disabilities who requires such assistance;
    d. the failure to provide medical and rehabilitative care for the physical and mental health needs of a high-risk adult with disabilities; or
    e. the failure to protect a high-risk adult with disabilities from health and safety hazards.

    Nothing in subsection 10 shall be construed to impose a requirement that assistance be provided to a high-risk adult with disabilities over his or her objection in the absence of a court order, nor to create any new affirmative duty to provide support to a high-risk adult with disabilities.

11. **Petitioner** may mean not only any named petitioner for the order of protection and any named victim of abuse on whose behalf the petition is brought, but also any other person protected by this Act.

12. **Physical abuse** includes sexual abuse and means any of the following:
    a. knowing or reckless use of physical force, confinement or restraint;
    b. knowing, repeated and unnecessary sleep deprivation; or
    c. knowing or reckless conduct which creates an immediate risk of physical harm.

13. **Stalking** means a person knowingly engages in a course of conduct directed at a specific person, and they know or should know that this course of conduct would cause a reasonable person to fear for their safety or the safety of a third person; or suffer other emotional distress.

14. **Willful deprivation** means willfully denying a person who because of age, health or disability requires medication, medical care, shelter, accessible shelter or services, food, therapeutic device, or other physical assistance, and thereby exposing that person to the risk of physical, mental or emotional harm, except with regard to medical care or treatment when the dependent person has expressed an intent to forgo such medical care or treatment. This paragraph does not create any new affirmative duty to provide support to dependent persons.

COURT'S WRITTEN FINDINGS:

After reviewing the *Petition* and hearing the evidence and testimony of Petitioner, the Court finds that:

1. ☐ **RULINGS PURSUANT TO** 750 ILCS 60/221(a)(2) and (b)(2)

   ☐ The relief requested in Sections: ☐ 2 ☐ 3 ☐ 10 ☐ 11 ☐ Other _____

   in the *Petition* is **denied** because the balance of hardships does not support the granting of the remedy; the granting of the remedy will result in hardship to Respondent that would substantially outweigh the hardship to Petitioner from the denial of the remedy; or because:

   _____
   _____
   _____

   ☐ The relief requested in the following sections are **reserved**:

   _____

2. Petitioner is related to Respondent in the following way *(check all that apply)*:

   ☐ Current or past dating relationship (BG)

   ☐ Have children together; never married (CC)

   ☐ Has or allegedly has a child together

   ☐ Related through current or past marriage:
   - ☐ Spouse (SE)
   - ☐ Ex-Spouse (XS)
   - ☐ In-law (IL)
   - ☐ Step-Child (SC)
   - ☐ Step-Brother / Step-Sister / Step-Sibling (SS)
   - ☐ Other Family Member (OF)

   ☐ Sharing or have shared a home (CS)

   ☐ Related through blood:
   - ☐ Child (CH)
   - ☐ Parent (PA)
   - ☐ Brother / Sister / Sibling (SB)
   - ☐ Grandchild (GC)
   - ☐ Grandparent (GP)
   - ☐ Other Family Member (OF)

   ☐ Has a blood relationship through a child

   ☐ Has a family or household relationship with a child who is the:
   - ☐ adoptive, prospective adoptive, or foster child of the Petitioner; or
   - ☐ of whom the Petitioner is the legal guardian or custodian

   ☐ Personal caregiver of the Petitioner, who has disabilities or who otherwise needs care

3. ☐ Respondent has received notice of Petitioner's request for an *Order of Protection*.

   ☐ Respondent has not received notice of Petitioner's request for an *Order of Protection*.

   ☐ Petitioner is present in person in court. ☐ Represented by: _____
   Name of Lawyer

4. ☐ Respondent is not present in court.

   ☐ Respondent is present in person in court. ☐ Represented by: _____
   Name of Lawyer

5. ☐ Good cause exists to grant these remedies in this *Order* even though Respondent has not received notice Because:

   ☐ a. If Respondent were given prior or greater notice, it is likely that the harm that the remedies in this *Order* are intended to prevent would occur (R01, R03, R05, R08, R09, R11, R14, R15, and R17).

   ☐ b. If Respondent were given prior or greater notice, the immediate danger of further abuse outweighs the hardships to Respondent of an *Order* granting exclusive possession of the residence (R02).

   ☐ c. If Respondent were given prior or greater notice, it is likely that personal property would be disposed of improperly, or Petitioner has an immediate and pressing need for possession of that property.

6. Other Relevant Factors and Findings (*check all that apply*):

☐ An *Order of Protection* has previously been entered in this case or in another case in which any party, or a child of any party has been named as either Respondent or Petitioner.

☐ An abused person is unable to bring this *Petition* on their own behalf due to age, health, disability, or inaccessibility.

☐ The *Petition* has been filed on behalf of a high-risk adult with disabilities who has been abused, neglected, or exploited by a family or household member.

☐ The Petitioner believes that the Respondent is (check all that apply): ☐ armed ☐ dangerous ☐ suicidal.

7. ☐ In granting the remedies in this *Order*, the Court has considered all relevant factors, including: the nature, severity, pattern, and consequences of Respondent's past abuse, neglect, or exploitation of Petitioner or any family/household member, including Respondent's concealment of their location in order to evade service of notice, and the likelihood of danger of future abuse, neglect, or exploitation to Petitioner or any member of Petitioner's or Respondent's family or household; and the danger that any minor child(ren) will be abused, removed from the jurisdiction, improperly concealed within the State, or improperly separated from the child(ren)'s primary caretaker. The court finds that:

o The Court has jurisdiction over Petitioner, Respondent, minor children and other Protected Persons.

o Venue is proper.

o Respondent has abused Petitioner and/or the children identified as protected persons in Section 5 on page 5 and/or the Protected Persons listed on page 1 of this *Order*.

o The actions of Respondent will likely cause irreparable harm or continued abuse unless they are prohibited.

o It is necessary to grant the requested relief in this *Order* to protect Petitioner or other abused persons.

8. ☐ **Criminal Cases:** The Court is entering this *Order* based on the following prima facie evidence (check all that apply):

☐ an information, complaint, indictment or delinquency petition, charging a crime of domestic violence or charging an attempt to commit a crime of domestic violence; or

☐ an adjudication of delinquency, a finding of guilt based upon a plea, or a finding of guilt after a trial for a crime of domestic battery; or

☐ any disposition order issued under Section 5-710 of the Juvenile Court Act of 1987, the imposition of supervision, conditional discharge, probation, periodic imprisonment, parole, aftercare release, or mandatory supervised release for a crime of domestic violence or an attempt to commit a crime of domestic violence, or imprisonment in conjunction with a bond forfeiture warrant; or

☐ the entry of a protective order in a separate civil case brought by Petitioner against Respondent.

ORDER OF PROTECTION

☐ Agreed   ☐ Modified   ☐ Extended

IN THE STATE OF ILLINOIS, CIRCUIT COURT

COUNTY: _____
County Where You Are Filing the Case

Enter the case information as it appears on your other court documents.

PETITIONER: _____
Who started the case.   *First, Middle, and Last Name*

Filing on behalf of a ☐ minor or ☐ high-risk adult: _____

RESPONDENT: _____
Who you are seeking protection from.   *First, Middle, and Last Name*

Case Number

People to be Protected by this *Order*:

Check the boxes for **all** people you want to include in the *Order*

☐ Petitioner: _____

☐ Petitioner's minor children with Respondent:

_____

_____

☐ Petitioner's other minor children:

_____

_____

☐ Dependent adult: _____

☐ High-risk adult: _____

☐ Other household members: _____

_____

_____

Civil Proceeding:
☐ Interim
☐ Plenary

Related Civil Case Number (if known)

Criminal Proceeding:
☐ Final

Related Criminal or Delinquency Case Number (if known)

ORDER INFORMATION:

☐ This *Order* was issued on: _____ at _____ ☐ a.m. ☐ p.m.
    Month, Day, Year   *Time*

☐ This *Order* will end on: _____ at _____ ☐ a.m. ☐ p.m.
    Month, Day, Year   *Time*

☐ This *Order* will end as entered on page 12.

☐ **NEXT COURT DATE:**

There will be a ☐ status ☐ hearing on:

_____ at _____ ☐ a.m. ☐ p.m. in _____.
Month, Day, Year   *Time*   *Courtroom Number*

Look at page 2 for more information on how to attend court.

This form is approved by the Illinois Supreme Court and must be accepted in all Illinois Courts. Forms are free at *ilcourts.info/forms*.
ATJ 405.4   Page 1 of 16   (05/25)

Court dates may be scheduled in-person, remotely, or a combination of in-person and remotely. Find out how your court date will be scheduled and provide that information here. Add the Clerk's phone number and website.

Attend court any of the ways checked:

☐ **In person** at: _____
             Courtroom Address   *Courtroom Number*

☐ **Remotely** *(video or telephone option)*

    By video conference at: _____
                         Video Conference Website

    Log-in information: _____
                Video Conference Log-in Information, Meeting ID, Password, etc.

    By telephone at: _____
                 Call-in Number for Telephone Remote Appearance

To find out more about remote court options:

Phone: _____ or Website: _____
     Circuit Clerk's Phone Number   *Website URL*

On the following issues:

_____

☐ Petitioner ordered to bring the following documents:

_____

☐ Respondent ordered to bring the following documents:

_____

> **Petitioner:** Note, if you are completing this form for a minor child, a dependent adult, or a high-risk adult, insert information needed below as if you were that person. In other words, do not use your information.

A. Petitioner's ☐ **residential address** or ☐ **alternative address for notice** (residential address is undisclosed)

_____
  Street, Apt #   *City*   *State*   *ZIP*

_____
  Email

B. Respondent's Information *(if known)*:

Date of Birth: _____ Sex: _____ Race: _____

Respondent's Home address:

_____
  Street, Apt #   *City*   *State*   *ZIP*

Respondent's Email: _____

Respondent's work information, including when usually works:

_____   _____
  Respondent's Employer Name   *Respondent's Work Hours*

_____
  Respondent Employer Street Address   *City*   *State*   *ZIP*

Other Respondent identifiers:

_____ _____ _____ _____
Height   Weight   Hair Color   Eye Color

Does the Respondent have any distinguishing features like scars, marks, or tattoos?

_____

THE COURT ORDERS THAT YOU OBEY ALL SECTIONS SELECTED BELOW:

☐ **1. No Abuse** **(R01) (Police Enforced)**

Respondent shall not threaten or commit the following acts of abuse towards Petitioner and protected people. *(check all that apply)*:

☐ Harassment   ☐ Intimidation of a Dependent
☐ Physical Abuse   ☐ Exploitation of a High-Risk Adult with Disabilities
☐ Stalking   ☐ Neglect of a High-Risk Adult with Disabilities
☐ Willful Deprivation   ☐ Interference with Personal Liberty

☐ **2. Possession of Residence** **(R02) (Police Enforced)**

Petitioner is granted exclusive possession of the residence and Respondent is ordered not to stay or be at the residence. These remedies do not affect who owns the property, only who gets to use or occupy it.

Petitioner's residence is located at *(check one)*:

    ☐ Petitioner's address is confidential and omitted from these forms.

or

☐ _____
      Street, Apt #   *City*   *State*   *ZIP*

The court finds:

    ☐ Petitioner has a right to occupy the residence and Respondent has no right; or
    ☐ Petitioner and Respondent both have the right to occupy the residence, but it would be harder on the Petitioner to leave after considering the factors set forth in 750 ILCS 60/214(b)(2)(B) or 725 ILCS 5/112A-14(b)(2)(B).

☐ Respondent shall provide alternate housing for Petitioner as follows:

_____

☐ **3. Stay Away from Petitioner, Protected People, and Certain Places** **(R03) (Police Enforced)**

    ☐ Respondent shall stay away from Petitioner and protected people at all times, and shall not have any contact, including through third parties.

> **Respondent:** If ordered to stay away from Petitioner and protected people, you (Respondent) must not have ANY physical, non-physical, direct, or indirect contact with Petitioner and protected people. This includes oral communication, written communication, sign language, telephone and cell phone calls, faxes, texts, tweets, emails, posts, or communication by any other social media, and all other communication with Petitioner and protected people. This also includes contact or communication through others who may not know about the *Order of Protection*.

☐ Respondent shall not be at or stay at any of these places while Petitioner is there:

    ☐ Places of employment of Petitioner, located at:

_____   _____
Name   *Street Address*   *City*   *State*   *ZIP*
                               or ☐ Address is confidential and is omitted from these forms.

_____   _____
Name   *Street Address*   *City*   *State*   *ZIP*
                               or ☐ Address is confidential and is omitted from these forms.

☐ Schools, kindergartens, or daycare centers of Petitioner, located at:

_____	_____			
Name	*Street Address*	*City*	*State*	*ZIP*

or ☐ Address is confidential and is omitted from these forms.

_____	_____			
Name	*Street Address*	*City*	*State*	*ZIP*

or ☐ Address is confidential and is omitted from these forms.

☐ Other locations:

_____	_____			
Name	*Street Address*	*City*	*State*	*ZIP*

or ☐ Address is confidential and is omitted from these forms.

_____	_____			
Name	*Street Address*	*City*	*State*	*ZIP*

or ☐ Address is confidential and is omitted from these forms.

☐ School Restrictions
Fill in only if Respondent attends the same school as Petitioner.

_____ is an elementary, middle, or high school
School Name attended by both Respondent and Petitioner.

After considering the factors in 750 ILCS 60/214(b)(3)(B):

☐ Respondent shall not attend this school for as long as Petitioner is enrolled there;
☐ Respondent shall accept a change of placement or program at this school as determined by the public school district or by this private or non-public school; OR
☐ Respondent shall follow these restrictions on movement within the school:

_____
_____
_____

☐ Requirements for Parents and Guardians
Respondent is a minor. To ensure that Respondent follows this *Order*, Respondent's Parent or Guardian:

_____
Name of Parent or Guardian
must do the following: _____
_____

☐ **4. Counseling** **(R04) (Police Enforced)**

Respondent must do the following and file proof with the Circuit Clerk by _____:
(check all that apply) *Date*

☐ Enroll in and successfully complete a Domestic Violence Partner Abuse program.
☐ Get an alcohol and substance abuse evaluation and complete recommended counseling or treatment.
☐ Get a mental health evaluation and complete any recommended counseling or treatment.
☐ Other: _____

INFORMATION ABOUT CHILDREN IN COMMON (SECTIONS 5-9)

NOTE: Legal parentage of a child may be established in the following ways: 1) There is a presumption of parentage because the parties are or were married or civilly united and the child was born during the marriage/union, within 300 days of its termination, or before the marriage/union and both parents' names have been added to their birth certificate. 2) Both parties have signed a Voluntary Acknowledgement of Paternity (VAP). 3) There is a court order or administrative order establishing parentage. 4) By giving birth to the child

Child's Name *(first, middle, last)*	Age	State of Residence	Legal Parentage Already Established for Petitioner (P) / Respondent (R)			Included as a Protected Person	
_____	___	_____	☐ - P	☐ - R ☐ Unsure		☐ Yes	☐ No
_____	___	_____	☐ - P	☐ - R ☐ Unsure		☐ Yes	☐ No
_____	___	_____	☐ - P	☐ - R ☐ Unsure		☐ Yes	☐ No
_____	___	_____	☐ - P	☐ - R ☐ Unsure		☐ Yes	☐ No
_____	___	_____	☐ - P	☐ - R ☐ Unsure		☐ Yes	☐ No
_____	___	_____	☐ - P	☐ - R ☐ Unsure		☐ Yes	☐ No

☐ The court finds the primary caretaker of the minor children is *(check one)*:
If the primary caretaker of the children is someone other than you or Respondent, check the box for "Other person" and enter that person's name and address.

☐ Petitioner ☐ Respondent
☐ Other person:

_____
Name of Person　　　　Street, Apt #　　　　City　　　　State　　　　ZIP

☐ The court finds it does not have jurisdiction over the children.

☐ The court finds it has jurisdiction over the children because:

☐ The children have lived in Illinois for the past six (6) months or if the children are younger than six (6) months old, they have lived in Illinois since they were born.

☐ Petitioner lives in Illinois but someone else took the children out of Illinois within the past six (6) months. Before they were taken out of Illinois, the children lived here for at least six (6) months.

☐ The children are in Illinois because Petitioner fled here to avoid abuse in another state.

☐ Other: _____

☐ 5. **Care and Possession of Children**　　　　　　　　　**(R05) Police/Court Enforced**

☐ Petitioner is granted physical care and possession of the minor children.

☐ Respondent shall, personally or through a law enforcement agency as authorized by the court, return the minor children to the physical care of:

☐ Petitioner
☐ Other person:

_____
Name of Person　　　　Street Address, Apt #　　　　City　　　　State　　　　ZIP

☐ Respondent shall not remove the minor children from the physical care of Petitioner or from a school or childcare provider. The names of the schools or providers are:

_____
Name of School or Childcare Provider

Case Number _____

☐ Within 24 hours of this Order being entered, the Circuit Clerk shall send written notice of the Order to the following school, daycare, or health care providers:

Name of Place	*Street Address*	*City*	*State*
Name of Place	*Street Address*	*City*	*State*
Name of Place	*Street Address*	*City*	*State*

    ☐ For the safety of Petitioner, the name and location of the school or daycare is listed on the Confidential Name & Location of the School or Childcare Provider form.

☐ **6. Temporary Significant Decision-Making Responsibility** *(formerly custody)*   **(R06) (Court Enforced)**

The Court awards Petitioner all significant decision-making responsibility of the minor children that Petitioner and Respondent have together.

☐ **7. Respondent's Parenting Time** *(formerly visitation)* **with the Minor Children**   **(R07) (Court Enforced)**

Parenting time is:

☐ GRANTED for the Respondent *(without any restrictions listed below)*.

☐ RESERVED until a later hearing *(The Court does not make ANY decision on parenting time right now)*.

    ☐ Associated with family case: _____.

☐ DENIED *(No visits at all)*.

☐ RESTRICTED *(Visits with limits as listed below)*.

    If parenting time is DENIED or RESTRICTED, check the reasons below:

    Respondent is likely to *(check all that apply)*:

    ☐ Abuse or endanger the children during parenting time.

    ☐ Use parenting time to abuse or harass Petitioner, Petitioner's family, or household members.

    ☐ Improperly hide or detain the children.

    ☐ Act in a way that is not in the best interest of the children.

☐ Parenting time is GRANTED or RESTRICTED as follows *(check the box that applies)*:

    ☐ See attached parenting time schedule; OR

    ☐ The parenting time schedule is *(check all that apply, include a.m. or p.m.)*:

        ☐ Every _____ from _____ to _____
            Weekdays   *Time*   *Time*

        ☐ Each weekend OR ☐ Every other weekend as follows *(include a.m. or p.m.)*:

            ☐ from: _____ at _____ to _____ at _____
               Day of the Week   *Time*   *Day of the Week*   *Time*

        ☐ Parenting time is to begin on: _____
                      Month, Day, Year

        ☐ Holidays (include date and times):

        _____

        _____

    ☐ The person responsible for transportation of the children for parenting time is:

    _____
    Name

☐ Pickup for parenting time to take place at the following place:

_____   _____   _____   _____
Name of Place (if any)   *Street Address*   *City*   *State*

☐ Return from parenting time to take place at the following place:

_____   _____   _____   _____
Name of Place (if any)   *Street Address*   *City*   *State*

☐ Parenting time will take place at:

_____   _____   _____   _____
Name of Place (if any)   *Street Address*   *City*   *State*

☐ Parenting time will be supervised by: _____
        Name of Supervisor

who has filed or will file an *Affidavit of Parenting Time Supervisor* form with the court accepting responsibility and acknowledging accountability.

☐ Parenting time will be supervised at an official supervised visitation center *(if available)*:

_____
   Name of Visitation Center

☐ Respondent to return the children immediately at the end of parenting time to:

  ☐ Petitioner

  ☐ Person chosen by Petitioner: _____
                        Name of Person Chosen by Petitioner

> **Respondent:** Petitioner may, by law, deny you (Respondent) access to the minor children if, when you arrive for parenting time, you are under the influence of drugs or alcohol and constitute a threat to the safety and well-being of Petitioner or the minor children of Petitioner or you are behaving in a violent or abusive manner (750 ILCS 60/214(b)(7)).

☐ 8. **No Concealment or Removal of Children**   **(R08) (Police Enforced)**

Respondent shall not hide the minor children within the State or remove the children from Illinois.

☐ 9. **Order to Appear**   **(R09) (Court Enforced)**

Respondent shall appear ☐ alone ☐ with minor children at the Courthouse:

_____   _____   _____   _____
Name of Courthouse   *Street Address*   *City*   *State*

in Courtroom _____ on _____ at _____ ☐ a.m. ☐ p.m.
        Courtroom   *Date*   *Time*

to *(check all that apply)*:

  ☐ Prevent abuse, neglect, removal, or concealment of the children.

  ☐ Return the children to the custody or care of Petitioner.

  ☐ Permit a court-ordered interview or examination of the children or Respondent.

☐ **10. Possession of Personal Property** *(does not affect ownership of property)*   (R10) (Court Enforced)
   Petitioner's Property:
   ☐ Petitioner is awarded possession of this property:

   _____
   _____
   _____

   ☐ Respondent be ordered to give Petitioner
      ☐ all of the property listed above ☐ the following:

   _____
   _____
   _____

   ☐ property given to _____.
                              Name of Person
   The Court finds as follows:
      ☐ Petitioner, but not Respondent, owns the property; or
      ☐ Petitioner and Respondent both own the property. Sharing it would put Petitioner at risk for abuse, or is
         not practical. Not having the property would be harder on Petitioner; or
      ☐ Petitioner claims the property as marital property, and a divorce case has been filed.

   ☐ Property shall be transferred at the following address:

   _____
   Street, Apt #   *City*   *State*   *ZIP*

   on _____ at _____ ☐ a.m. ☐ p.m.
        Month, Day, Year   *Time*
   ☐ Property shall be transferred only in the presence of:
      ☐ Law enforcement to be arranged by Petitioner

         (Optional) ☐ _____ ;
                          Name of Law Enforcement Agency
      or
      ☐ Another adult: _____
                          Name

Respondent's Property
   ☐ Respondent is awarded possession of the following personal property: ☐ clothing ☐ medicine
   ☐ other personal property as follows:

   _____
   _____
   _____

   ☐ Respondent shall have the right to enter the residence listed in Section **2** <u>only one time</u> to retrieve the
      property listed above, but only in the presence of: (check one)
      ☐ Law enforcement to be arranged by Respondent

         (Optional) ☐ _____ ;
                          Name of Law Enforcement Agency
      or
      ☐ Another adult: _____
                          Name

☐ **11. Restrictions on Property** **(R11) (Court Enforced)**

The Respondent shall not take, transfer, encumber, conceal, hide, damage, or otherwise dispose of any real or personal property, except as explicitly authorized by the Court. The following property is protected:

☐ Cars/Motor Vehicles (*Specify Make/Model/Year*): _____

☐ Address: _____

   <u>Street, Apt #</u>   <u>City</u>   <u>State</u>   <u>ZIP</u>

   ☐ Inside/Outside
   ☐ Items located inside

☐ Other important property:

_____

_____

BECAUSE *(check one)*:

☐ Petitioner, but not Respondent, owns the property.
☐ Petitioner and Respondent both own the property. Not having the property would be harder on Petitioner.
☐ The parties are married and a divorce case has been filed.

☐ Restrictions on Resources of an Elderly Petitioner
Respondent is prohibited from improperly using financial or other resources of an elderly Petitioner for the benefit of Respondent or any other person.

☐ **11.5 Possession of Animals** **(R11.5) (Court Enforced)**

Petitioner shall have care, custody, and control over the following animals (*include name, type and breed*):

_____

_____

Respondent shall stay away from the animals and Respondent is forbidden from taking, transferring, concealing, harming, or otherwise disposing of the animals.

☐ **12. Temporary Support** **(R12) (Court Enforced)**

The Court finds that Respondent is: ☐unemployed   ☐self-employed   ☐employed by:

_____

<u>Name</u>   <u>Street Address</u>   <u>City</u>   <u>State</u>   <u>ZIP</u>

and has approximate net pay in the amount of: $_____   ☐ weekly   ☐ every two weeks
                                                               ☐ twice a month ☐ monthly

The Court finds that Petitioner is: ☐unemployed   ☐self-employed   ☐employed by:

_____

<u>Name</u>   <u>Street Address</u>   <u>City</u>   <u>State</u>   <u>ZIP</u>

and has approximate net pay in the amount of: $_____   ☐ weekly   ☐ every two weeks
                                                               ☐ twice a month ☐ monthly

☐ Respondent shall pay temporary **child support** to Petitioner in the amount of $_____

☐ weekly   ☐ every two weeks   ☐ twice a month   ☐ monthly

☐ Payments shall begin on: _____ and shall continue until further order of the Court.
                              <u>Date</u>

☐ Respondent shall pay temporary **support** (maintenance) to Petitioner in the amount of $_____

☐ weekly   ☐ every two weeks   ☐ twice a month   ☐ monthly

☐ Payments shall begin on: _____ and shall continue until further order of the Court.
                              <u>Date</u>

Payments shall be made:

☐ Through the Circuit Clerk:
    ☐ Child Support ☐ Temporary Support (maintenance)

☐ Through the State Disbursement Unit (SDU) (Fill out separate *Order of Support*):
    ☐ Child Support ☐ Temporary Support (maintenance) *(SDU will only take maintenance with child support.)*

☐ Directly to Petitioner by this method of payment _____:
    ☐ Child Support ☐ Temporary Support (maintenance)

☐ **13. Payment for Losses because of Abuse.** **(R13) (Court Enforced)**

Respondent shall pay Petitioner for losses suffered as a direct result of abuse, neglect, or exploitation, including:

☐ Medical expenses.. $_____
☐ Lost earnings.. $_____
☐ Repair or replace property damaged or taken.. $_____
☐ Moving and other travel expenses.. $_____
☐ Reasonable expenses for housing other than a domestic violence shelter........................ $_____
☐ Expenses for search and recovery of children... $_____
☐ Reasonable attorney's fees... $_____
☐ Other: _____ $_____

☐ The total amount of: $_____ by _____
                                  Date

☐ Payments in the amount of: $_____ every _____ starting _____.
                                                  Frequency   *Date*

☐ Method of payment: _____.

☐ **14. No Entry or Presence Under Influence** **(R14) (Police Enforced)**

Respondent is allowed at the Petitioner's residence but cannot be or stay there while under the influence of drugs or alcohol. Respondent constitutes a threat to the safety of Petitioner or Petitioner's children:

_____
Street Address, Apt #   *City*   *State*   *ZIP*

Respondent: Under Illinois law, while any Order of Protection is in effect, your (Respondent's) FOID card will be automatically suspended, revoked or denied and you are automatically prohibited from acquiring or possessing a firearm (per 430 ILCS 65/8.2). Your conceal and carry license is also suspended while the Order is in effect and must be turned over to the Court or law enforcement (per 430 ILCS 66/70B).

When an Order ends, you can request the return of your firearms and FOID card as long as your FOID card is not expired and there is no other order restricting your possession of firearms.

☐ **14.5. Firearms**   **(R14.5) (Police Enforced)**

Respondent is prohibited from possessing firearms for the duration of this order. Respondent must immediately surrender to law enforcement (and not transfer to a third party) any firearms, firearm parts that could be assembled to make an operable firearm, Firearm Owner Identification (FOID) Card, and/or Concealed Carry License. If these items are not in Respondent's possession at time of service, they must be surrendered to law enforcement (and not transferred to a third party) within 24 hours.

The Court finds as follows:

Civil Orders:

☐ Respondent has received actual notice of this request and has had an opportunity to participate.

☐ This order restrains Respondent from using physical force, harassment, stalking, or threatening an intimate partner or child of an intimate partner.

☐ Respondent poses a credible threat to the physical safety of Petitioner.

☐ Probable cause exists to believe that:

    ☐ Respondent possesses firearms or firearm parts that could be assembled to make an operable firearm.

    ☐ The firearms or firearm parts that could be assembled to make an operable firearm are located at the residence, vehicle, or other property of the Respondent.

    ☐ The credible threat to the physical safety of Petitioner is immediate and present.

☐ Petitioner has made a credible report of domestic violence to local law enforcement within the last 90 days.

Criminal Orders:

☐ Respondent is subject to this domestic violence order of protection and may not lawfully possess firearms, firearm parts, or a FOID card under Section 8.2 of the Firearm Owners Identification Act.

☐ Probable cause exists to believe that:

    ☐ Respondent possesses firearms or firearm parts that could be assembled to make an operable firearm.

    ☐ The firearms or firearm parts that could be assembled to make an operable firearm are located at the residence, vehicle, or other property of the Respondent.

    ☐ Respondent poses an immediate and present credible threat to Petitioner.

☐ **15. Children's Records**   **(R15) (Court Enforced)**

Respondent is not allowed to access, inspect, or obtain school records or any other records of the minor children in the care of Petitioner because *(check all that apply)*:

    ☐ This *Order of Protection* prohibits Respondent from having contact with the minor children.

    ☐ The actual address of Petitioner is not included due to the risk of further abuse.

    ☐ It is necessary to prevent abuse or wrongful removal or concealment of the minor children.

☐ **16. Shelter Reimbursement.**   **(R16) (Court Enforced)**

Respondent shall pay $_____ to _____

                                         Shelter Name

by _____ for the cost of services and shelter provided to Petitioner.

    Date

☐ **17. Miscellaneous Remedies**   **(R17) (Court Enforced)**

The court further orders as follows:

_____

_____

_____

_____

_____

☐ **18. Telephone Services** **(R18) (Court Enforced)**

After considering the evidence, the wireless telephone service provider shall terminate Respondent's use of Petitioner's phone number, transfer to Petitioner the right to use these phone numbers, and transfer to Petitioner all financial responsibility associated with future use of these phone numbers.

Wireless telephone provider account details:

Name of Provider: _____

Name of Account Holder: _____

Respondent's Phone Number: _____

Petitioner's Phone Numbers: _____

_____

STOP **Petitioner: STOP! Only the Judge or Circuit Clerk should enter anything below this point.**

☐ **RULINGS PURSUANT TO** 750 ILCS 60/221(a)(2) and (b)(2)

☐ The relief requested in Sections: ☐ 2 ☐ 3 ☐ 10 ☐ 11 ☐ Other: _____
in the *Petition* is **denied** because the balance of hardships does not support the granting of the remedy; the granting of the remedy will result in hardship to Respondent that would substantially outweigh the hardship to Petitioner from the denial of the remedy; or because:

_____
_____
_____

☐ The relief requested in the following sections are **reserved**:

_____

PLENARY *(FINAL)* ORDERS ONLY:
If no specific date for expiration is entered on page 1, this *Order* will remain in effect as follows:

☐ **1. Until further order of the Court (only by extension or by special findings)**

☐ **If entered in conjunction with another civil proceeding:**

☐ 2. If entered as preliminary relief, until entry of final judgment in the other proceeding.*

☐ 3. If incorporated into the final judgment of the other proceeding, until the Order is vacated or modified.*

☐ 4. Upon termination of any voluntary or involuntary commitment, or on _____.
Date (Not to Exceed 2 Years)

☐ **If entered in conjunction with a criminal prosecution or delinquency petition pursuant to 725 ILCS 5/112A-20:**

☐ 5. If entered during pre-trial release until disposition, withdrawal, or dismissal of the underlying charge.
○ Sets of disposition means: not guilty, which would include dismissal, nolle pros, or finding of not guilty.
○ For finding or pleading of guilty, see sections 7 or 8 and complete a new order.

☐ 6. Until final disposition when a Bond Forfeiture Warrant has issued, or on _____.
Date (Not to Exceed 2 Years)

☐ **If entered with a finding of guilty:**

☐ 7. Until expiration of any supervision, conditional discharge, probation, periodic imprisonment, parole, or supervised mandatory release, plus 2 years.*

☐ 8. Until 2 years after the date set by the court for expiration of any sentence for imprisonment, parole, and mandatory supervised release.*
This Order may last more than two years if entered in conjunction with a civil or criminal proceeding.

After reviewing the *Petition* and hearing the evidence, the Court makes findings which:

☐ Are written on page 15 and 16 of this *Order*;

☐ Were made orally and videotaped or recorded by a court reporter and are incorporated into this *Order*; or

☐ The parties have agreed to this Order and no additional findings are made.

ENTERED:

_____   _____
Judge   Date

I hereby certify that this is a true and correct copy of the original order on file with the Court.

Clerk of the Circuit Court of _____ County, Illinois _____
                                                                                                                                Date

_____
Seal (and signature, as locally required)

Copies given to: ☐ Petitioner ☐ Respondent in Open Court ☐ State's Attorney

Clerk to send copies to Sheriff to: ☐ serve Respondent

☐ enter into LEADS

Order drafted by

Attorney: _____
                  Name   Address   Telephone   Attorney Number (if any)

Notices About Enforcement:

A violation of this order may result in fine or imprisonment.

Any knowing violation of an *Order of Protection* forbidding physical abuse, neglect, exploitation, harassment, intimidation, interference with personal liberty, willful deprivation, or entering or remaining present at specified places when any Protected Persons are present, or granting exclusive possession of the residence or household or granting a stay away order is a crime. Grants of exclusive possession of the residence or household shall constitute notice forbidding trespass to land. Any knowing violation of an order awarding parental responsibility (formerly custody) or physical care of a child or care of a child or prohibiting removal or concealment of a child may be a crime. Any willful violation of any order is contempt of court.

This *Order of Protection* is enforceable with notice to the Respondent, even without registration, in all 50 states, the District of Columbia, tribal lands, and the U.S. Territories pursuant to the Violence Against Women Act (18 U.S.C. § 2265),. Violating this *Order of Protection* may subject the Respondent to state and/or federal charges and punishment. 18 U.S.C. §§ 2261-2262.

DEFINITION OF TERMS USED IN THIS *ORDER*

1. **Abuse** means physical abuse, harassment, intimidation of a dependent, interference with personal liberty or willful deprivation but does not include reasonable direction of a minor child by a parent or person in loco parentis.
2. **Adult with disabilities** means an elder adult with disabilities or a high-risk adult with disabilities. A person may be an adult with disabilities for purposes of this Act even though he or she has never been adjudicated an incompetent adult. However, no court proceeding may be initiated or continued on behalf of an adult with disabilities over that adult's objection, unless such proceeding is approved by his or her legal guardian, if any.
3. **Elder adult with disabilities** means an adult prevented by advanced age from taking appropriate action to protect himself or herself from abuse by a family or household member.
4. **Exploitation** means the illegal, including tortious, use of a high-risk adult with disabilities or of the assets or resources of a high-risk adult with disabilities. Exploitation includes, but is not limited to, the misappropriation of assets or resources of a high-risk adult with disabilities by undue influence, by breach of a fiduciary relationship, by fraud, deception, or extortion, or the use of such assets or resources in a manner contrary to law.
5. **Family or household members** include spouses, former spouses, parents, children, stepchildren and other persons related by blood or by present or prior marriage, persons who share or formerly shared a common dwelling, persons who have or allegedly have a child in common, persons who share or allegedly share a blood relationship through a child, persons who have or have had a dating or engagement relationship, persons with disabilities and their personal assistants, and caregivers as defined in Section 12-4.4a of the Criminal Code of 2012. For purposes of this paragraph, neither a casual acquaintanceship nor ordinary fraternization between 2 individuals in business or social contexts shall be deemed to constitute a dating relationship. In the case of a high-risk adult with disabilities, "family or household members" includes any person who has the responsibility for a high-risk adult as a result of a family relationship or who has assumed responsibility for all or a portion of the care of a high-risk adult with disabilities voluntarily, or by express or implied contract, or by court order.
6. **Harassment** means knowing conduct which is not necessary to accomplish a purpose that is reasonable under the circumstances; would cause a reasonable person emotional distress; and does cause emotional distress to the petitioner. Unless the presumption is rebutted by a preponderance of the evidence, the following types of conduct shall be presumed to cause emotional distress:
    a. creating a disturbance at petitioner's place of employment or school;
    b. repeatedly telephoning petitioner's place of employment, home or residence;
    c. repeatedly following petitioner about in a public place or places;
    d. repeatedly keeping petitioner under surveillance by remaining present outside his or her home, school, place of employment, vehicle or other place occupied by petitioner or by peering in petitioner's windows;
    e. improperly concealing a minor child from petitioner, repeatedly threatening to improperly remove a minor child of petitioner's from the jurisdiction or from the physical care of petitioner, repeatedly threatening to conceal a minor child from petitioner, or making a single such threat following an actual or attempted improper removal or concealment, unless respondent was fleeing an incident or pattern of domestic violence; or
    f. threatening physical force, confinement or restraint on one or more occasions.
7. **High-risk adult with disabilities** means a person aged 18 or over whose physical or mental disability impairs his or her ability to seek or obtain protection from abuse, neglect, or exploitation.
8. **Interference with personal liberty** means committing or threatening physical abuse, harassment, intimidation or willful deprivation so as to compel another to engage in conduct from which she or he has a right to abstain or to refrain from conduct in which she or he has a right to engage.
9. **Intimidation of a dependent** means subjecting a person who is dependent because of age, health or disability to participation in or the witnessing of: physical force against another or physical confinement or restraint of another which constitutes physical abuse as defined in this Act, regardless of whether the abused person is a family or household member.
10. **Neglect** means the failure to exercise that degree of care toward a high-risk adult with disabilities which a reasonable person would exercise under the circumstances and includes but is not limited to:
    a. the failure to take reasonable steps to protect a high-risk adult with disabilities from acts of abuse;
    b. the repeated, careless imposition of unreasonable confinement;
    c. the failure to provide food, shelter, clothing, and personal hygiene to a high-risk adult with disabilities who requires such assistance;
    d. the failure to provide medical and rehabilitative care for the physical and mental health needs of a high-risk adult with disabilities; or
    e. the failure to protect a high-risk adult with disabilities from health and safety hazards.

    Nothing in subsection 10 shall be construed to impose a requirement that assistance be provided to a high-risk adult with disabilities over his or her objection in the absence of a court order, nor to create any new affirmative duty to provide support to a high-risk adult with disabilities.
11. **Petitioner** may mean not only any named petitioner for the order of protection and any named victim of abuse on whose behalf the petition is brought, but also any other person protected by this Act.
12. **Physical abuse** includes sexual abuse and means any of the following:
    a. knowing or reckless use of physical force, confinement or restraint;
    b. knowing, repeated and unnecessary sleep deprivation; or
    c. knowing or reckless conduct which creates an immediate risk of physical harm.
13. **Stalking** means a person knowingly engages in a course of conduct directed at a specific person, and they know or should know that this course of conduct would cause a reasonable person to fear for their safety or the safety of a third person; or suffer other emotional distress.
14. **Willful deprivation** means willfully denying a person who because of age, health or disability requires medication, medical care, shelter, accessible shelter or services, food, therapeutic device, or other physical assistance, and thereby exposing that person to the risk of physical, mental or emotional harm, except with regard to medical care or treatment when the dependent person has expressed an intent to forgo such medical care or treatment. This paragraph does not create any new affirmative duty to provide support to dependent persons.

COURT'S WRITTEN FINDINGS:

After reviewing the *Petition* and hearing the evidence and testimony of Petitioner, the Court finds that:

1. Petitioner is related to Respondent in the following way *(check all that apply)*:

☐ Current or past dating relationship (BG)

☐ Have children together; never married (CC)

☐ Has or allegedly has a child together

☐ Related through current or past marriage:
   ☐ Spouse (SE)
   ☐ Ex-Spouse (XS)
   ☐ In-law (IL)
   ☐ Step-Child (SC)
   ☐ Step-Brother / Step-Sister / Step-Sibling (SS)
   ☐ Other Family Member (OF)

☐ Sharing or have shared a home (CS)

☐ Related through blood
   ☐ Child (CH)
   ☐ Parent (PA)
   ☐ Brother / Sister / Sibling (SB)
   ☐ Grandchild (GC)
   ☐ Grandparent (GP)
   ☐ Other Family Member (OF)

☐ Has a blood relationship through a child

☐ Has a family or household relationship with a child who is the:
   ☐ adoptive, prospective adoptive, or foster child of the Petitioner; or
   ☐ of whom the Petitioner is the legal guardian or custodian

☐ Personal caregiver of the Petitioner, who has disabilities or who otherwise needs care

2. ☐ Respondent has received notice of Petitioner's request for an Order of Protection.
☐ Respondent has filed an answer or appearance.
☐ Respondent has been notified through publication.
☐ Respondent is not present in court and is in default.
☐ Respondent is present in person in court. ☐ Represented by: _____
                                                             Name of Lawyer
☐ Petitioner is present in person in court. ☐ Represented by: _____
                                                             Name of Lawyer

3. In granting the remedies in this *Order*, the Court has considered all relevant factors, including: the nature, frequency, severity, pattern, and consequences of Respondent's past abuse, neglect, or exploitation of Petitioner or any family/household member, including Respondent's concealment of their location in order to evade service of process or notice, and the likelihood of danger of future abuse, neglect, or exploitation to Petitioner or any member of Petitioner's or Respondent's family or household; and the danger that any minor child(ren) will be abused, neglected, or improperly removed from the jurisdiction, improperly concealed within the State, or improperly separated from the child(ren)'s primary caretaker. The Court finds that:

   o The Court has jurisdiction over Petitioner, Respondent, minor children and other Protected Persons.

   o Venue is proper.

   o Respondent has abused Petitioner and/or the children identified as protected persons in Section 5 on page 5 and/or the Protected Persons listed on page 1 of this *Order*.

   o The actions of Respondent will likely cause irreparable harm or continued abuse unless they are prohibited.

   o It is necessary to grant the requested relief in this *Order* to protect Petitioner or other abused persons.

4. Other Relevant Factors and Findings (*check all that apply*):

☐ An *Order of Protection* has previously been entered in this case or in another case in which any party, or a child of any party has been named as either Respondent or Petitioner.

☐ An abused person is unable to bring this *Petition* on their own behalf due to age, health, disability, or inaccessibility.

☐ The *Petition* has been filed on behalf of a high-risk adult with disabilities who has been abused, neglected, or exploited by a family or household member.

☐ The Petitioner believes that the Respondent is (check all that apply): ☐ armed ☐ dangerous ☐ suicidal

5. ☐ **Criminal Cases:** The Court is entering this *Order* based on the following prima facie evidence (check all that apply):

☐ an information, complaint, indictment or delinquency petition, charging a crime of domestic violence or charging an attempt to commit a crime of domestic violence; or

☐ an adjudication of delinquency, a finding of guilt based upon a plea, or a finding of guilt after a trial for a crime of domestic battery; or

☐ any disposition order issued under Section 5-710 of the Juvenile Court Act of 1987, the imposition of supervision, conditional discharge, probation, periodic imprisonment, parole, aftercare release, or mandatory supervised release for a crime of domestic violence or an attempt to commit a crime of domestic violence, or imprisonment in conjunction with a bond forfeiture warrant; or

☐ the entry of a protective order in a separate civil case brought by Petitioner against Respondent.

SUMMONS

(PROTECTIVE ORDERS)

IN THE STATE OF ILLINOIS, CIRCUIT COURT

☐ **Alias Summons**

Check if this is not the 1ˢᵗ Summons issued for this Respondent.

COUNTY: _____

County Where You Are Filing the Case

Enter the case information as it appears on your other court documents.

PETITIONER: _____

Who started the case.   First, Middle, and Last Name

Filing on behalf of a ☐ minor or ☐ high-risk adult: _____

RESPONDENT: _____

Who you are seeking protection from.   First, Middle, and Last Name

_____

Case Number

- ○ A case has been filed against you. Read all of the documents attached to this Summons.
- ○ To participate in the case, you must follow the instructions listed below. Also see page 3 for next steps.
- ○ You **must attend court** on the date in this Summons. If you do not attend that date or on any subsequent hearing date agreed to by the parties or set by the court, the judge may decide the case without hearing from you. This is called "default."
- ○ All documents referred to in this Summons can be found at ilcourts.info/forms. Other documents may be available from your local Circuit Court Clerk's office or website.

1. Petitioner has filed against you for the following:

☐ Order of Protection   ☐ Stalking No Contact Order

☐ Civil No Contact Order   ☐ Other: _____

2. Instructions for person receiving this form (Respondent):

Your court date is listed below. Information about getting a court date and how to attend is available from the Circuit Clerk. You can find their contact information at ilcourts.info/clerks.

☐ Go to court on the date in the attached Order.

☐ Go to court in one of the ways checked below on:

_____ at _____ ☐ a.m. ☐ p.m. in _____.

Month, Day, Year   *Time*   *Courtroom Number*

Court dates may be in-person, remote, or a combination of in-person and remote.

☐ **In person** at: _____

Courtroom Address   *Courtroom Number*

☐ **Remotely** (video or telephone)

By video conference at: _____

Video Conference Website

Log-in information: _____

Video Conference Log-in Information, Meeting ID, Password, etc.

By telephone at: _____

Call-in Number for Telephone Remote Appearance

To find out more about remote court options:

Phone: _____ or Website: _____

Circuit Clerk's Phone Number   *Website URL*

This form is approved by the Illinois Supreme Court and is required to be accepted in all Illinois Circuit Courts. Forms are free at ilcourts.info/forms.

ATJ 502.6   Page 1 of 5   (05/25)

81

3. RESPONDENT'S INFORMATION

a. Respondent's **primary address/information** for service:

Name: _____
First, Middle, and Last Name, or Business Name

Street Address: _____
Street, Apt #

City, State, ZIP: _____
City   *State*   *Zip*

Telephone: _____ Email: _____

b. **Second address** for this Respondent:

☐ I do **not** have another address where the Respondent might be found.

☐ I have another address where this Respondent might be found. It is:

Street Address: _____
Street, Apt #

City, State, ZIP: _____
City   *State*   *Zip*

Telephone: _____ Email: _____

c. Person who will serve your documents on this Respondent:

☐ Sheriff in Illinois ☐ Special process server ☐ Licensed private detective

☐ Sheriff outside Illinois: _____
County & State

PETITIONER INFORMATION FOR NOTICE PURPOSES:

Enter your complete address, telephone number, and email address if you have one. If you need to keep your addresses secret because of domestic violence, you may use another address. Those addresses must be ones at which you can receive mail about the case.

Name: _____
First, Middle and Last Name

Street Address: _____
Street, Apt #

City, State, ZIP: _____
City   *State*   *Zip*

Telephone: _____ Email: _____

Be sure to **check your email every day** so you do not miss important information, court dates, or documents from other parties.

STOP   The Circuit Clerk and officer or process server will fill in this section.

To be filled in by the Circuit Clerk:

Witness this Date: _____   *Seal of Court*

Clerk of the Court: _____

To be filled in by an officer or process server:

Date of Service: _____

Fill in the date above and give this copy of the Summons to the person served.

Note to officer or process server:

o Complete the attached *Proof of Service* form and file it with the court or return it to the Petitioner.

WHAT'S NEXT

NEXT STEPS FOR PERSON FILLING OUT THIS FORM:

When you file a case, you must notify the Respondent of the court case by having the *Summons* and *Petition for Order of Protection* delivered to them. This is called "serving" them.

File your *Summons* and *Petition* with the Circuit Clerk in the county where your court case should be filed. The Circuit Clerk will "issue" the *Summons* by putting a court seal on the form.

Have the sheriff or a private process server serve the *Summons* and a copy of the *Petition* and *Order* (if entered) on the Respondent. You cannot serve the *Summons* yourself.

Learn more about each step in the process and how to file in the instructions: ilcourts.info/OP-summons-instructions.

NEXT STEPS FOR PERSON RECEIVING THIS DOCUMENT:

A case has been filed against you:

- Read all documents attached to this *Summons*.
- All documents referred to in this *Summons* can be found at ilcourts.info/forms. Other documents may be available from your local Circuit Court Clerk's office or website.
- Within 7 days of receiving this Summons you must file a document called an *Appearance*. If you do not file required court documents on time, the judge may decide the case without hearing from you. This is called "default." As a result, you could lose the case and a protective order could be entered against you. You do not have to file a document called an Answer/Response in a protective order case unless ordered to by the judge.
- After you fill out the necessary documents, you need to electronically file (e-file) them with the court. To e-file, you must create an account with an e-filing service provider. For more information, go to ilcourts.info/efiling. If you cannot e-file, you can get an exemption that allows you to file in-person or by mail.
- You may be charged filing fees, but if you cannot pay them, you can file an *Application for Waiver of Court Fees (Civil)*.
- When you go to court, it is possible that the court will allow you to attend the first court date in this case in-person or remotely by video or phone. Contact the Circuit Court Clerk's office or visit the Court's website to find out whether this is possible and, if so, how to do this.

Need Help? ¿Necesita ayuda?

- Call or text Illinois Court Help at 833-411-1121 or go to ilcourthelp.gov for information about going to court, including how to fill out and file documents.
- Llame o envíe un mensaje de texto a Illinois Court Help al 833-411-1121, o visite ilcourthelp.gov para obtener información sobre los casos de la corte y cómo completar y presentar formularios.
- You can also get free legal information and legal referrals at illinoislegalaid.org.
- If there are any words or terms that you do not understand, please **visit Illinois Legal Aid Online** at ilao.info/glossary. You may also find more information, resources, and the location of your local legal self-help center at: ilao.info/lshc-directory.

PROOF OF SERVICE OF SUMMONS
FOR PROTECTIVE ORDERS

IN THE STATE OF ILLINOIS, CIRCUIT COURT

☐ **Alias Summons**
Check if this is not the 1ˢᵗ Summons issued for this Respondent.

COUNTY: _____
County Where You Are Filing the Case

Enter the case information as it appears on your other court documents.

PETITIONER: _____
Who started the case.   First, Middle, and Last Name

Filing on behalf of a ☐ minor or ☐ high-risk adult: _____

RESPONDENT: _____
Who you are seeking protection from.   First, Middle, and Last Name

_____
Case Number

STOP Do not complete the rest of the form. **The sheriff or special process server will fill in the form.**

My name is _____ and I state:
Officer/Process Server First, Middle, Last Name

SERVICE INFORMATION

Respondent: _____
First, Middle, Last Name

☐ I was not able to serve the *Summons, Petition,* and *Orders* issued in this case on the Respondent named above.

- or -

☐ I served the *Summons, Petition* and *Orders* issued in this case on the Respondent named above as follows:

☐ **Personally** on the Respondent:

☐ Male ☐ Female ☐ Non-Binary Approx. Age: _____ Race: _____

On this date: _____ at this time: _____ ☐ a.m. ☐ p.m.

Address, Unit#: _____

City, State, ZIP: _____

☐ On **someone else at the Respondent's home** who is at least 13 years old and is a family member or lives there:
Name of person served: _____
First, Middle, Last Name

☐ Male ☐ Female ☐ Non-Binary Approx. Age: _____ Race: _____

On this date: _____ at this time: _____ ☐ a.m. ☐ p.m.

Address, Unit#: _____

City, State, ZIP: _____
and by sending a copy to this Respondent in a postage-paid, sealed envelope to the above

address on this date: _____.

This form is approved by the Illinois Supreme Court and is required to be accepted in all Illinois Circuit Courts. Forms are free at ilcourts.info/forms.
ATJ 502.6   Page 4 of 5   (05/25)

SERVICE ATTEMPTS

I made the following attempts to serve the *Summons* and Petition on the Respondent:

First Attempt: On this date: _____ at this time: _____ ☐ a.m. ☐ p.m.

Address, Unit#: _____

City, State, ZIP: _____
Other information about service attempt:

_____

_____

_____

Second Attempt: On this date: _____ at this time: _____ ☐ a.m. ☐ p.m.

Address, Unit#: _____

City, State, ZIP: _____
Other information about service attempt:

_____

_____

_____

Third Attempt: On this date: _____ at this time: _____ ☐ a.m. ☐ p.m.

Address, Unit#: _____

City, State, ZIP: _____
Other information about service attempt:

_____

_____

_____

SIGN

I certify under 735 ILCS 5/1-109 that:

1) everything in this document is true and correct, or I have been informed or I believe it to be true and correct, and

2) I understand that making a false statement on this document is perjury and has penalties provided by law.

Your Signature /s/ _____ Print Your Name _____

You are: ☐ Sheriff in Illinois   ☐ Special process server
☐ Sheriff outside Illinois: _____ ☐ Licensed private detective, license number: _____
County and State   *License number*

FEES:

Service and Return: $_____ Miles: $_____ Total: $_____

SEARCH WARRANT FOR
SEIZURE OF FIREARMS
(ORDER OF PROTECTION)
IN THE STATE OF ILLINOIS, CIRCUIT COURT

COUNTY: _____
County Where You Are Filing the Case

Enter the case information as it appears on your other court documents.

PETITIONER: _____
Who started the case.   *First, Middle, and Last Name*

RESPONDENT: _____
Who you are seeking protection from.   *First, Middle, and Last Name*

Case Number _____

This form is used by the Judge to issue a search warrant for seizure of firearms, firearm parts, Firearms Owner's Identification Card (FOID), and Concealed Carry Licenses pursuant to 750 ILCS 60/214-14.5(A-1) or 725 ILCS 5/112A-14(b)(14.5)(B-1).

Use one *Search Warrant for Seizure of Firearms* for each location, building or vehicle needing to be searched.

To _____ and all peace officers of the State of Illinois:
Law Enforcement Agency

Petitioner, _____, has been sworn under oath and testified before the court.
Petitioner's name

The Court finds that Petitioner's testimony shows that there is probable cause that:

☐ Respondent poses an immediate and present credible threat to the physical safety of Petitioner

☐ Respondent possesses a firearm or firearm parts that could be used to make a firearm; and

☐ The firearm or firearm parts are in the residence, vehicle, or other property of Respondent.

Petitioner ☐ has not ☐ has made a credible report of domestic violence to local law enforcement within the last 90 days.*

The Court therefore orders a search of the property listed below for the seizure of any of the following items in the possession of or belonging to Respondent, _____:
Respondent's name

☐ Firearms   ☐ Firearm parts that could be assembled to make an operable firearm

☐ FOID cards   ☐ Concealed Carry Licenses

☐ Other: _____
Specify items to be seized

Property to be searched (including the particular scope of the search):

_____

_____

_____

_____

The Court further orders that a return of this warrant with the time, date, and location where the warrant was executed and what items, if any, were seized be filed within 24 hours of execution of this warrant.

ENTERED:

_____   _____   _____
Judge   *Date (Month, Day, Year)*   *Time (am or pm)*

*Civil only: If a report of domestic violence within the previous 90 days, law enforcement shall execute the warrant no later than 96 hours after receipt. If there has not been a report, law enforcement shall, within 48 hours of receipt, evaluate the warrant and seek any corrections to the warrant.

This form is approved by the Illinois Supreme Court and must be accepted in all Illinois Courts. Forms are free at ilcourts.info/forms.

ATJ 412.1   Page 1 of 1   (05/25)

NAVIGATING THE WINDING ROAD

FAMILY LAW AND ESTATE PLANNING IN ILLINOIS

By Gwendolyn J. Sterk and the Family Law Group, P.C.

Gwendolyn J. Sterk
and the Family Law Group, P.C.

Empower Yourself With Options.

Dear Duke... My Parents Are Getting Divorced

Pawsitive Ideas for Children Going Through a Divorce

By Duke Sterk™ & K.P. Lynne

www.ingramcontent.com/pod-product-compliance
Lightning Source LLC
Chambersburg PA
CBHW081140090426
42736CB00018B/3423